DO YOU STILL LIKE FOOTBALL

From Harley-Riding Rancher to Fashion Icon:
A Journey of Courage and Reinvention

Andrea Leigh

Do You Still Like Football

From Harley-Riding Rancher to Fashion Icon:
A Journey of Courage and Reinvention

Published by Soulful HBW, LLC
www.andrealeigh.com

Andrea Leigh

Bible Psalm from the New International Version.

First paperback edition January 2025

ISBN: 979-8-9912324-0-1

Foreword by Linda Fisk

Cover photography by Tia Dawn Photography

Cover design by 99designs.com

To Summer,

*I'm sorry for taking him from you. Thank
you for accepting me in return.*

To my parents,

*Thank you for telling me God had a plan for me
and setting me off with the wind at my back.*

CONTENTS

FOREWORD

D o You Still Like Football by Andrea Leigh is a must-read, providing an enlightening education on the personal struggles, profound decisions, and personal consequences of transitioning.

In this extraordinary memoir, Andrea weaves through her personal reflections, thoughtful considerations, and weighty decisions about her gender and body, her precipitous path to being the woman that she envisioned, and the turmoil of relationships on an emotional, romantic, and spiritual plane, culminating in a book that is as tender as it is profound. At times surprising, humorous, and deeply moving, Andrea explores the territory that lies between men and women, examines changing friendships and relationships, and rejoices in the redeeming power of love and family.

Andy was happily married to a beautiful ballerina named Summer, and together they were raising a young daughter in an idyllic family life. Andy was a competitive triathlete and successful rancher in Oklahoma, and enjoyed a comfortable lifestyle, providing for his family in multiple sales divisions within the pharmaceutical industry. All Andy ever wanted was a stable life, and after meeting the love of his life and marrying her a few years later, he was leading the life of which he had always dreamed. But after all the successes, achievements, and triumphs left him still searching for more, he listened to a call from the inside. Through a series of procedures, sometimes humorously detailed in this book, he transformed and became Andrea Leigh.

In the process, Andrea reinvented herself from the ground up, moving to a new neighborhood, changing careers, and beginning a whole new life. In many ways, this book is a memoir of a life spent pursuing and achieving the American Dream, while keeping buried the truth of her own gender identity, until, finally, Andrea turned to face who was staring back in the mirror. A marvel of grace and empathy, *Do You Still Like Football* parses with great sensitivity many issues that touch our lives deeply, of gender identity and far beyond. Both a fascinating memoir of a well-educated, successful man with rich family relationships making the decision to pursue the tricky waters of a gender change, and an honest and candid introspective of the impact of that decision, *Do You Still Like Football* asks us to reconsider our knee-jerk reaction to gender categorization.

This groundbreaking book offers deep insight for anyone seeking to understand the internal journey. Andrea thoughtfully shares the mental and emotional processes she navigated while candidly detailing how she reimagined, redesigned, and rebuilt her life. Her story provides a window into the courage and resilience required for such a profound transformation, offering both inspiration and understanding for readers at every stage of personal growth. The reader is invited to follow the intimate journey of Andrea and her family, as they learn to survive and then ultimately embrace transition, turning their story into an inspirational roadmap for others living through similar situations. *Do You Still Like Football* tells the story of a family learning to accommodate and then embrace transition. In the process, they unwittingly become role models for others facing the uncertainties of change.

Andrea's story is both deeply personal and also inspirational and encouraging. Whether it's her efforts in collaborating with her wife and daughter through her transition, alerting her co-workers of her decision, or taking the painstaking steps to prepare herself and others, her story is sure to resonate with the reader.

Do You Still Like Football opens a door to a new understanding of gender and identity with compassion, sincerity, and vulnerability. It offers an informative and empowering story of love, acceptance and the desire to live life authentically with confidence and strength.

AUTHOR'S NOTE

In this memoir, I share my personal journey, including my experiences with hormone replacement therapy (HRT) during my gender transition. In one chapter, I reference an arm of the Women's Health Initiative, or WHI study (https://www.whi.org/), which evaluated the effects of combined estrogen and progestin hormone replacement therapy on postmenopausal women. I have purposefully simplified the explanation of the WHI findings to avoid any potential contention or misinterpretation. While this arm of the study conclusions had significant implications for the use of HRT, the hormone dosages I take regularly are far higher than those used in the WHI study, and I use different forms of these hormones.

This book is my personal reflection on the journey I've taken, and I want to clarify that the information provided in these sections is not intended as medical advice, nor is it a critique of the pharmaceutical industry. My goal is to share my story in a way that resonates with readers while respecting the complexity of medical research and its interpretations.

WHAT HAVE YOU DONE TO YOURSELF?

The procedure was to have lasted four to five hours. It had already been five. Dr. Nuveen finally walked out. "Andrea is in recovery. She did well." Handing the woman waiting two prescriptions, he said, "You need to fill these. She will need these as she recovers."

For hours, she had waited alone. I was now finished and could awake at any time. Frustrated, she immediately left so as to be back before then. Frustrated that the first pharmacy didn't have both medications on hand, she had to fill the second in a "dicey part of town."

Returning to the center and using a key for the back door, she entered the area set aside for patients being held overnight. A bedroom with a sofa, hospital bed, and bathroom sat next to the kitchen area for the clinic. After informing the staff that she had come back, she settled in again. She didn't have to wait long. Dr. Nuveen returned and found her on the sofa. Following behind, I was in a wheelchair pushed by one of the nurses. With my head wrapped in bandages front to back and top to bottom, I was slumped forward, unable to hold my head up. My hands and arms shook uncontrollably, and Summer was scared. Scared for both of us. She was scared for me, my well-being, and scared for herself. She would be left alone to care for me that night.

What have you done to yourself? she thought.

It would be another rough eighteen hours.

BARRY SWITZER AVENUE

The house was located on Barry Switzer Avenue in Norman, Oklahoma. The street was named after the three-time national championship football coach at the University. It was one of the first homes shown to me on my first day house shopping. Touring the house, I was met with a brick entryway that led into a beautiful kitchen, bricked on one side, with a built-in grill and range top. But none of that mattered. The street was named after Barry Switzer, one of the winningest coaches in college football history. The former head coach of the Oklahoma Sooners. The home belonged to the departing offensive coordinator, who was leaving for a head coaching job of his own. I wanted that address. My offer was made and accepted quickly.

I have been a Sooner football fan and loved football for as long as I can remember. The football schedule and games all weekend would signal the change in season that would bring cool weather, my birthday, and the holidays. My whole life seemed to be scheduled around the sport. My family watched Oklahoma football on Saturdays. The Dallas Cowboys and Oakland Raiders would cause family feuds that forced my mother out of the house every Sunday. Monday Night Football finished off each week of the season, leading us to a four-day break for school, work, and chores.

As a little boy, I collected football cards and read the statistics on the back of each card to my mother as she worked in the kitchen.

"Mom, guess how many yards passing Roger Staubach had last year?"

"You'll have to tell me" she would respond. She knew it was important to me.

"Mom, can you believe how big Art Shell is?"

"How big is he?"

"Dick Butkus wants to tear a guy's head off," I said, laughing.

"He's not as good as Ray Nitschke," Dad chimed in.

For years, these conversations were normal.

I met Switzer on a junior high school field trip to Norman. Exiting the door that we were walking into, he greeted us with, "Hey boys, how you all doing?" We were thrilled, and he gave us time, attention, and autographs.

When Switzer took the head coaching job for the Dallas Cowboys, the local news station came to Barry Switzer Avenue and interviewed me along with some of my neighbors for the evening news. Holding my daughter's hand, we appeared on that night's broadcast, showing our excitement. I kept the recording of that news broadcast for years. Switzer's thoughts on success and winning would be highly influential throughout the course of my life, personally and professionally. Switzer's saying, "There is no limit to your success if you don't care who gets the credit," has been a guiding principle through my life both at home and at work.

***

I had been in that house over eight years, the last four as a single parent trying to maintain a promising young career in the healthcare and pharmaceutical industry. My first marriage had failed after six years. My ex-wife and I maintained a relationship centered on giving our daughter a life with both of us and our families. Most evenings with my daughter after the workday ended consisted of finishing the household chores and getting dinner ready for both of us. I was a great cook and made dinner from scratch most of the time. We would clean the kitchen and head off into the living room. Sports on television, particularly football, dominated most of the programming. We would follow our favorite teams as one season ended and another began. It was easy for me to maintain this routine. Bathing my daughter most evenings and setting her to bed with her books left me with a couple of hours to decompress before it was lights out. It was a great time for us.

Yet I still wanted a repeat of the life I had experienced with my parents. I wanted this for my daughter. I wanted nothing more than a "normal" family again. I now realize how remarkably special those first twenty years were for me. At the time, though, I hadn't yet realized that we were far from normal … and what a blessing that "not normal" had been.

I soon got what I wished for: a coworker introduced me to a woman that checked every box for what I believed I wanted for myself and my daughter. We hit it off. Dating and engaged within months, I sold my '95 Corvette convertible. My family of three wouldn't need a two-seater. But months after that, it was over. We had met, dated, engaged, married, and separated in less than ten months.

I had seen the red "warning lights" early and thought I could change them. The lights never changed. The marriage soon descended into a living hell. When we separated, being alone again, after this fiasco, was welcomed with tears. Tears of joy. Being alone was better than being with the wrong person. To make matters worse, I had missed a whole season of football because she hated the sport.

There is no such thing as normal. I would never care about being normal again.

One gorgeous spring day after the separation, I picked up my daughter from day care, drove home, and unloaded the car. I had worked all day visiting rural Oklahoma hospitals and clinics. I had joined the company two years before, after leaving my first job in the industry with a severance package during a planned reorganization. These restructures would become common in the industry over the next twenty years. I unlocked the front door and turned around to go check the mailbox by the road. My daughter walked into the house. She came back out and asked, "Where is all the furniture?"

"What are you talking about?"

I walked inside the house. It was gutted; emptied of everything that wasn't mine before the second marriage. We had acquired a lot in those few short, turbulent months, and now it was all gone. The woman had come back months after she'd left to deliver one more blow to us. The coworker had tipped her off as to when I would be out of town working. My eyes went over the empty rooms. In the living room was a lone chair and a television for the two of us. I stood in the entry as if my life in the house was just beginning again. I looked at the footprints of the missing furniture, and smiled. I realized life could very well begin again. I grabbed my keys, looked at my daughter, and said, "Let's go."

"Where are we going?"

"To get some furniture," I answered. It was just stuff.

Within a couple of hours, I had replaced the same pieces that had been taken from the living room. When the delivery men arrived with it the next day, they asked where I wanted the furniture placed. I found it humorous to say, "Right there in the footprints for each piece." My daughter and I sat in the kitchen, hugged, and cried. The nightmare for both of us was over.

It took a day to replace the furniture. But that Corvette, it had been sold months before in the mistaken belief that someone else could make me happy. Setting that belief system right was now in progress. I would fill my life with more experiences than I could imagine for the next two decades and beyond.

Those ten turbulent months were an amazing life experience. It was a "blip." But that blip would lead me to appreciate selfless love when it presented itself later.

2000 OKLAHOMA SOONERS

UNDEFEATED NATIONAL CHAMPIONS
13 - 0

EXPERIENCES

My daughter and I worked at making up for that lost year of experiences immediately. The two of us began by going to San Diego for a relaxing vacation. Visits to the San Diego Zoo, SeaWorld, and the Old Town Neighborhood were broken up by relaxing days reading beside the pool at one of the Marina Bay hotels, and evenings of fine dining around the city. She would swim; I would lie in the sun and read one of the four to five books brought along on the trip. Tan, rested, and ready, we headed back to Oklahoma. Experience number one was behind us.

We had missed the entire previous football season. Oklahoma wasn't looking so awful anymore; previous seasons had been embarrassing for the fans and the program. New head coach Bob Stoops had brought a new attitude with a "no excuses" mindset. I had season tickets to the games for close to twenty years, which I'd attended long before I was a student at the school. As the fresh season got underway, OU just kept winning. Big wins against conference rivals Texas, Kansas State, and Nebraska returned Oklahoma to the top of the college football rankings. My daughter and I attended most of the games at home and on the road. The football fever was intense with the fans and the resurgent program. This easily made up for us having missed the previous season.

As the football season wound down, my daughter's ballet classes were well underway. She had taken instruction in classical ballet for four years. My younger sister, Erin, had danced as a child and I wanted a similar activity for my daughter that would occupy her as I finished my workday, worked out, or simply kept her away from the video screen that dominated children of that age. Her instructor at the studio had been a ballerina at the University of Oklahoma and had taught her since her initial enrollment. Summer Cooper, a Native American Indian of the Creek and Seminole tribes, had been associated with or attended the school of dance at OU since she was five years old. Paying for her own educational costs through waitressing, work at the movie rental store, or shifts at the bakery in town, she demonstrated a work ethic that I hadn't seen in any of girls I had ever known or dated. But it was familiar to me from my family, and I liked it. The instruction she gave the children was kind and direct. They were budding dancers after spending one academic year with her. She was and still is a natural teacher.

Waiting for my daughter to get dressed after class that fall, I caught "Miss Summer" off guard and asked if she would like to go out.

"I'm working," she replied, as if I meant at that very instant.

"Well, I don't mean right now," I responded, laughing.

In recalling our initial interactions, Summer later revealed, "I thought you were handsome, a good dad, super friendly, and I had told my boss that you would marry me. You asked me to go out and then waited two weeks to call me."

When I finally did make that call, we went for burgers at a local favorite in Norman. We followed that up with a Sooner basketball game in the evening.

The football season concluded with the Sooners playing Florida State in the Orange Bowl for the national championship. My daughter and I made a trip to the game, which ended with a Sooner victory and a return to glory for the program. A season of experiences had ended beautifully. God, I loved football. I called Summer. In Oklahoma, if you were a fan, you took ownership of the results of your team. It was her first national championship.

Three months later, the kid and I were headed to Texas for the NASCAR races at Texas Motor Speedway. The Texas 500 was on the schedule, and the company sponsored the number 6 car. I was one of the point people promoting a new drug in Oklahoma. The product had been on the market for two years, and the company had just contracted to sponsor the race team for the next several seasons. I had been given tickets to the race to share with my clients. We would provide them with the most current information on the product and enjoy the race experience with them afterwards.

It was the loudest sporting event or concert that I had ever attended. Headphones were crucial to maintaining one's hearing. From our seats, any form of verbal communication was next to impossible for the duration of the race. The super speedway tracks are immense in size, and the afternoon walk to the car after the race wiped us out. Crossing the Red River back into Oklahoma, we stopped to enjoy fried catfish with a client, his wife, and sons. Daddy-Daughter experience number three was behind us.

Two months after the race, we found ourselves in Tulsa for the US Open Golf Championship held at Southern Hills. The company was a major sponsor and again we were given tickets to share with our clients. We would educate and entertain them before heading to the course as the foursomes got underway. One of the number 6 cars was on display at the event.

As the educational portion ended, the last client was put on the shuttle to the course for round one. My daughter and I were left with the car. The crew was ready to trailer it. They asked her if she wanted to sit in it. The biggest smile I had seen in years crossed her face as she enthusiastically accepted. Crawling out the window afterwards, she watched the car get loaded for travel, still beaming.

I grabbed her hand and we left for the course. We checked in and headed to the sponsor tents. Dropping our belongings at the company tent, we continued to the range, stopping at the practice bunkers. Tiger Woods was in the sand. There wasn't a much better experience for a seven-year-old or her dad to have at this time than to see Tiger Woods up close practicing his bunker play before he headed off to make his tee time. It brought great joy to the two of us see him that first morning.

The summer days in Oklahoma can be hot and humid, and this day was no exception. We found a shaded spot around a green and watched the different foursomes come through and play the hole. Eventually, we made our way back to the sponsor tent to cool down and eat ice cream bars before heading out to the course one last time. We found the most shaded hole on the course. It was a par three. Phil Mickelson was in the next group as we prepared to leave for the day. We decided we would watch for a bit longer, although it was so hot and we still had a two-hour drive home ahead of us. He came to the tee and hit the ball beautifully, right into the cup. A hole-in-one. The eruption of the crowd to this shot by one of the greats was an experience neither of us would forget. Seeing Mickelson's genuine joy up close was special. I was so excited for my daughter to be there.

Finally, it was time to go. Thirty minutes up close with Tiger and Mickelson's ace in the Open … chalk up another great experience.

I called Summer on the way back to Oklahoma City. Her happiness for us and our experience was authentic. She was the real deal, and our experiences together had not even started yet.

I had started something new with the ballerina. The previous fiasco of a marriage would ensure that I wasn't missing anything. I just needed the time to know it.

2001 OKLAHOMA SOONERS

COTTON BOWL CHAMPIONS
11 - 2

WYNNEWOOD

My impressive start to a new job took an unexpected turn after eighteen months. Eighteen months marked the end of a probationary period that company representatives had to pass through to continue their careers with the industry giant.

The company's representatives have been long considered to be at the top of a competitive industry, and the training standards were set to maintain that belief. I needed to go to Dallas and prove that I should be kept as an asset to the company. It was an intensive session with the management team and a host of guest trainers.

My team in Oklahoma received a call from the regional office. The manager that had hired me into my current role had suddenly left the company and the team was left with little direction. Another teammate and I were to make the trip to Dallas together and needed to present our individual business results and plans to upper management in a few weeks.

These presentations are created as a team and practiced over and over with teammates. Pharma is like a sports competition; hires are made and careers are started based on the prospects for future results. These presentations were like big games, and careers were broken at this juncture. I had relied on someone else to have prepared me with the game plan, and that someone was no longer with the company. I knew I had talent, however. And I thought I knew my business.

We were welcomed to Dallas with a great dinner hosted by the boss. Sitting at dinner, all the guests would engage in small talk and feign enthusiasm for the time spent with the host. It was exhausting hanging on every his every word and watching our p's and q's. As we waited for our dinner to arrive, he had a guest trainer sing "The Girl From Ipanema" for us. It felt like a scene from a movie where the king says, "Dance, jester, dance." I was embarrassed. The corporate dinners always lasted too long because no one wanted to be the first to leave. When they finally did end, it was usually late with something important the next morning. That was the case here.

Sales presentations from those of us under scrutiny were scattered throughout the following day. Mock presentations to mock committees, and role plays with primary care physicians and cardiologists, were graded by the management and guest trainers. Our product expertise and disease state knowledge was tested and reviewed thoroughly over the two days. Finally, we presented our state-of-business data. I watched multiple presentations from my counterparts and knew I was in deep shit. One after another, they were excellent examples of using PowerPoint presentations to highlight completely unique geographical business models. I knew my business, but was ill-prepared to present it visually. I could and did present; but the data was in my head, not on a high-tech display. Nothing of note made any visual impact. My teammate had the same experience.

The final day was a formality. We were brought to the offices for our results. I received rave reviews for my sales technique, presentations to the mock committees, and role plays. I passed the science and academic portion with flying colors. One by one, we were then brought to the boss's office. I sat across from him at his desk with absolutely no idea of where this was headed. I had sat in the same office a little over a year before and been given a choice of building business for the company in Oklahoma City or San Antonio. It was Oklahoma City or bust. I was a single parent with joint custody. I wasn't leaving my daughter.

"The business review was not up to our level of expectation. We are not passing you on," my boss stated. I was devastated. Before I could say anything, he added, "We want to see you come back and give that presentation again. Just the presentation, no tests or sales techniques."

I was going to get a do-over. My technical preparations had gone out the door with the manager, and they knew it.

I left Dallas with mixed feelings. I had just lost big at a pivotal career point. But I wasn't eliminated from the game yet. This was one of my first times to realize that in a professional setting, one succeeds or learns. I learned. Fast.

Before returning to repeat the ordeal, upper management joined me for a day spent visiting my local clients. A pleasant day of driving rural Oklahoma was broken up by stops at multiple clinics to give sales presentations so headquarters could have feedback on what my relationships were like in the field. Pulling our presentation material from the car at one point, the boss commented, "Nice shoes."

They were. The brown snakeskin lace-ups looked beautiful under the navy suit.

The review of my rapport with clients wouldn't be as scrutinized as my shoes were that day. My observers understood what real relationship selling looked like at ground level. I had the gift and they knew it. I loved the relationships I had established since joining the organization. My rapport was excellent. I'm glad I wore the navy suit and the brown snakeskin lace-ups. It was my fashion that was being complimented as I was under review. My fashion. How appropriate and what nice foreshadowing.

Back to Dallas for the rematch. I repeated the presentation, this time with a PowerPoint slide deck to match my knowledge and delivery. I would not underperform again my entire career. Two others with similar circumstances after our presentation experience had been offered the same opportunity and chose to leave the company for new careers instead. I was praised for just showing up a second time. Most candidates quit.

A Rookie of the Year Award and my first Premier Award finished out the year. I knew my numbers and I understood my clients. I knew how to teach, deliver information, and be authentically myself in doing the job. I was driven to win. I would do it everywhere with great relationships.

***

A new manager moved to Oklahoma to lead the team, and my career entered a successful and comfortable phase. He was on a solo mission, following his own career path, taking advantage of the higher education benefit for his future endeavors; he kept the team off the radar. My days were smooth. When we did meet, the meetings were filled with games and food in the name of team-building. The company had gotten bloated, and it was apparent to me that the music would not go on forever. "Comfortable" isn't good for the growth of corporations or individuals.

The division was later taken to Orlando for the launch of a new combination medication. It was a combination of two of the best-selling cardiology agents on the market, both sold by the company. One was for reducing high cholesterol and the other was the top-selling branded medication for the treatment of high blood pressure. The marketing plan was unbelievably complicated. They were each top agents in their categories. It should've been simple. But patients that were currently taking both medications were off limits. The company wanted to continue the sale of both agents individually. The rest was a mess. Capture the patients currently on one of the two and add the other agent to whoever needed both kinds of treatment and prescribe them one pill. But switches from both specific meds to the combination? No.

A woman from the New York office assigned to the marketing campaign of this branded medication soon came to a conference with me and a few of my clients. We had established a nice relationship that morning as we connected on our shared experience of triathlon. As we drove through the countryside of Oklahoma, she turned and asked me, "What do you think of the Three Pillars Of Success?"

"The what?" I responded.

"The Three Pillars of Success."

"I have no idea what you're talking about."

"I told them this!" she yelled in frustration. "It's the marketing plan for this drug. I told them it was too complicated."

I turned to her. "It *is* too fucking complicated. I sell more of this than most anybody in this area of the country. Get the patient dialed in to the right dosages of each medication, then switch them to save money. Tell Madison Avenue that if they have questions to call and see if that shit will fly in Wynnewood, Oklahoma."

She laughed and said I would hear from her again. I didn't.

Pockets of the country did well with the "switch" strategy. Despite what I'd said, it wasn't complicated, really. It was a bad strategy. The company couldn't explain it coherently and the clients weren't buying into it. But it was too late to change direction. In the pharma industry, you only get one chance to launch a drug. This one failed on a national level. Doctors weren't going to buy into a drug with a marketing plan that simply didn't make sense.

The local team fell into mediocrity with a lack of direction to win. Individually, I maintained my career path and would begin to take it through multiple therapeutic divisions and compounds.

THE BALLERINA

The travel was significant in those first several years with the company: trainings, team and leadership meetings, and regular national product launches. The trips with my daughter took place in this same time frame. Summer's degree and work at the studio demanded her time. So we made time where we could for each other as often as we could.

We kept our relationship a secret from my daughter for months. She was seven, and trying to explain the relationship of Dad and her ballet instructor wasn't at the top of our priority list. Seeing each other on my ex-wife's weekends was normal, and during the week after bedtime wasn't unusual. I was thankful my daughter could sleep anytime and anywhere. Laughing and taking joy in each other's career, academic success, and getting through each week to the next weekend kept Summer and I going. We were going to Oklahoma basketball games and appreciating each other more every day.

The secrecy didn't last for more than a few months. My ex dropped the kiddo off at the house early one day while Summer and I were watching television in the living room. All of us were surprised, and best of all, experienced a congenial response to the circumstances. My ex enjoyed Summer and was pleased for the three of us.

I introduced Summer to my mother after the next ballet recital. It was a pleasant meeting, and I was proud of who I was dating. She's such a beautiful soul, I loved introducing her to everyone. We also ballroom danced for a talent show while on vacation with my extended family. Summer has such a wonderful spirit and she was easily accepted into the crew.

I was thirteen years older than Summer. I had two failed marriages behind me and a daughter. I was rapidly excelling in a rejuvenated career with little thought for the future beyond what was right in front of me. I had no vision established for myself except to save for retirement one day and live happily until that point. It was great to live in the present moment. I was either working out or playing golf after work day after day.

Summer had been working towards a degree in ballet pedagogy for the last several years. I recognized her work ethic. The degree was her way out of the way of life that many in her family let themselves believe was normal. The pride in their Native American heritage was apparent. The joy and happiness at family gatherings was contagious. The lack of individual responsibility in the culture for one's health, career choices, and upward mobility had been fostered by the government for over a century. Summer felt an intense desire to live differently than the rest of the family. This created tension that continually permeated her familial relationships. But they felt a loyalty to each other that bridged individual differences when times got tough. For many in the Native American community, that wasn't uncommon. But her future life path would be different than what she had seen travelled in her family.

We couldn't have been raised more different. We couldn't be more complementary.

***

In the spring of 2002, Summer sat on the floor in front of my desk in the office. Reviewing my finances and end-of-day reports, I started a conversation regarding our viewpoints on all things marriage-related. We discussed children, and the schooling of them, views on religion, the role of our parents and in-laws, and money. Our values were the same. We were very fond of each other, and in love. With no romance whatsoever, I asked Summer her thoughts on getting married. We thought it would be a good idea to continue our discussion over dinner. At an outdoor table over hamburgers, we decided we would do it.

Weeks later, I took the knee and gave her a beautiful ring in the ballet studio, where we had met several years before. The engagement went quickly, and we got married in December 2002. We honeymooned in Santa Fe, where we continue our getaway vacations to the present day.

We planned for children and swiftly met with success. Summer was pregnant during her last semester of school. Her capstone project would be on the subject matter of teaching ballet to pregnant women. She wrote the course and submitted accompanying video instruction that we worked to film together only months before our daughter was born. Walking across the stage eight months pregnant, she received her degree.

Summer made my house our home. She never seemed bothered with the knowledge that two other women had lived with me in that house. I have always been impressed with her confidence in the knowledge that we were made for each other.

2002 OKLAHOMA SOONERS

ROSE BOWL CHAMPIONS

12 - 2

I CAN'T GET UP

I'd long had a dedicated fitness regime, but after my marriage, I switched up my training to be home more with the family. I hated being away when I wasn't in the clinics. I still went to the gym for some strength training, but that was becoming a smaller part of my routine.

I had been enamored with the challenge of triathlon since watching numerous Ironman World Championships raced in Kona, Hawaii. My mother and I watched the prerecorded broadcasts of the race from our living room. NBC would present the struggles and stories of what the amateur athletes pushed themselves to accomplish, physically and mentally far beyond what was normal, just to complete the race. We followed their stories as they dragged themselves over the finish line. I wanted that, badly. Starting at zero and being able to finish an endeavor that relatively few people would ever attempt. I was motivated. But motivation, as I would learn and talk about later, could accomplish nothing. It was discipline, the ability to do what one does not want to do, that would be the factor in not just finishing, but having respectable times as I crossed the finish line. I actually needed to start, and thinking about it wasn't doing it.

I had been in the pool training in the recent past. I was a swimmer as a kid and was comfortable in the water. As part of my initial triathlon training before I met Summer, I would wake at 5:30, and be out of bed, in my suit, swimming at the University of Oklahoma pool in thirty minutes. I needed enough time to develop and maintain my swimming technique and fitness level before I showered, rushed home for breakfast, and got dressed and ready before anyone was up. I arrived in the clinics at the normal time, so my sense of loyalty and my work ethic didn't suffer.

A divorce and single parenting put an end to that endeavor. But with Summer, I could start swimming again. A training ride on the bike from the house during the week took an hour after work. I could leave the house for a 5k run and be back inside of thirty minutes. I committed. The time away from the family wasn't noticeable. Fitness had always been a priority so not much would change.

I had Summer's full support. But would I be disciplined enough to swim at the crack of dawn again, sometimes in damn cold water, bike in the Oklahoma wind after work, and run when I could? It was hard getting up at 5:30. Over time, however, waking, putting on my training suits, gulping a quick protein drink, and swimming laps got easier. In the cold, the heat, and the rain, discipline found me and was my friend for a very long time.

Three times a week in the pool was all I needed. Earlier bedtimes and better fitness developed over the next few months. Riding after work was comfortable. Too comfortable. I had biked long distance for years. Leaving my comfort zone to excel on the bike for triathlon was hard. I would struggle with that up to my last race.

Running through the university, around the fraternities and sororities, brought back so many memories. In college, I was initiated and lived as a member of the Sigma Phi Epsilon fraternity (where I still hold alumni status). I lived with the "brothers" and spent my days working for the girls of the Pi Beta Phi Sorority as a houseboy. I later found it humorous to tell people that I was one of the few women that had lived in a fraternity during college. Working as a houseboy for my meals was nothing to dream about at the time. But it was much better food than the fraternity provided, and it offered us a dose of reality of what our girlfriends really looked like upon waking when they came down for breakfast. The formal dinners for the Pi Phi house were opportunities to get a great meal, wear a waiter's coat, and rush to the girl's side when she raised her hand for new silverware or whatever else she might request. It had been twenty years, and I could still remember the parties the Greek system hosted during the year. Running these routes took little motivation, and I developed a great base for my longer distances later.

***

Valentine's Day.

Damn, it was cold. The schedule that I had meticulously created and followed called for a ninety-minute ride. I headed west on State Highway 9. It had a wide shoulder and the local community was at ease with bikers on the road. The ride was relatively flat for the first few miles, then changed to rolling hills as I ventured further outside of Norman and turned north.

I had mounted aero bars on my road bike. These bars allow cyclists to be down-positioned, ideal for cutting through the wind. Mounting these on a road bike was the cheap way to gain aerodynamic advantage, but the choice ended up being far more costly than I'd planned. The hips are placed in an aggressive angle, and the pressure on both the lower back and hips can be intense.

My nose was pouring snot due to the cold weather and I was beginning to not feel well. It took me forever to warm up. As I rode into the evening, powering up the hills, coasting down the backside to recover, I had to pace myself to get home. Country music star Toby Keith had a beautiful home along the route. I turned around at his place and headed back. Every iteration of climbing and descending after the turn felt horrible. That night, the flat last few miles home were brutal. Something wasn't right in my body.

It was dark and cold. I worried about getting run over and was grateful to finally turn into the neighborhood. I put the bike away, walked into the house, and stripped down to get warm. Nauseous, I showered and finally settled into the chair next to the warmth and glow of the fireplace.

That fireplace was a huge, brick, real wood fireplace, and the ambience it put off in the room was wonderful. I was relieved to be home and getting warm. Feeling rested and recovered, I tried to get up and go to the kitchen for a late dinner with Summer.

I couldn't move. At all. I attempted to stand up and was unable.

"You have to help me up," I said to Summer.

She braced herself, pulled me out of the chair, and helped me get across the room to the sofa. I stayed there for hours with my back in an intense spasm. Finally going to bed, I slept through the night, waking to get ready for a meeting with my boss and another colleague. Dressing in my suit and tie was a chore. I couldn't bend over to put on pants, socks, or shoes. Somehow, I made it to the meeting on time. Shuffling into the darkened hotel restaurant, I joined them for breakfast. I sat down, and in blinding pain, immediately stood up again.

I made my presence short-lived. I couldn't focus.

Afterwards, I pushed through pain for days that ran together. I would wake, shuffle to the shower, and dress for work. Before bed, I would place all the utensils, bowls, and plates for breakfast out for my convenience. The memories of making oatmeal and eggs each morning during that time will never fade. The pain was so intense, I would lie on the carpeted floor between stirrings of oatmeal for some relief. I finished breakfast, had my coffee, and would leave at the normal time. I could maintain focus for the short face-to-face meetings with the physicians.

It was still winter. The cold was brutal and made it difficult to maintain the heat around my lower back. Continuing to work and never improving, I let my physician know about my status. I was prescribed ibuprofen for some pain relief and any swelling that might be occurring. Healthcare providers were being inundated daily at this time with patients seeking prescriptions for pain meds. The difficulty for providers was discerning the difference in the pain thresholds of their patients and deciding what medications to use in each particular case. The drugs were so effective at relieving the physical pain, the resulting numbness to the rest of someone's life could be addicting as well. The physical effects from long-term usage could also be problematic. This is well known now, and most authoritative guidelines reflect this information. My personal physician was no different. The simple fact that I was continuing a normal routine led him to conclude that things couldn't have been too bad. Days later, with no progress, he ordered an MRI. I had attempted to maintain my training, but it was all but impossible. Triathlon would wait.

That MRI could not have arrived any sooner. This particular machine looked like a hamburger bun. Undressed and wrapped up like burrito, it felt good to lie on the surface of the scanner. It was dark and cool in the testing room, but I was warm, bundled up tight and placed between the "buns." They told me not to be startled by the banging of the magnets. I was just happy to be here being scanned for answers. The wheels of medicine are almost as slow as the wheels of justice. I was relaxed through the procedure, knowing the wheels were at least turning.

The test concluded. Dressed, I was about to head out of the center. It was dark in the monitoring room. I turned to the MRI tech who was reviewing images on the screen. "See anything?" I inquired.

"We let the doctors review the images and visit with you," she responded. But she had this wide-eyed look on her face.

I walked over to see the screen. She didn't cover it from my view as I reviewed the images of my spinal column in detail. Each alternating bony vertebra and the cushioning discs between were so detailed that anyone with a basic background in physiology could make out what I was seeing on the monitor. In this case, it was what I wasn't seeing. There was no disc between the L5-S1 vertebra in my lower back. "There is no disc there!" I exclaimed.

She shook her head. "No, there's not."

"You get this to the doctor fast!" I told her. I had known things weren't normal and now I'd had my suspicions confirmed.

My physician and I were high school classmates who had taken physiology together. He had graded out with an A, while I escaped the requirement with a D. We found that tidbit humorous later when we reconnected as a pharmaceutical representative and an internist. After seeing the MRI results myself, I didn't wait long before heading to his office.

I had access as a representative and headed straight back to his nurse's station. He came out of the exam room looking down at his files. He glanced up and saw me standing there in front of him. "I got your test results. I'm going to set you up with a neurosurgeon!" he declared.

My disc? It actually was there, misaligned and hard to find. The resulting pressure on the nerves of my spinal column was making my life miserable.

I felt vindicated. He finally understood. "I told you this wasn't normal."

He wrote me a prescription for something stronger than ibuprofen and passed me off to the specialist.

***

I was advised that I would need surgery, and we scheduled the procedure for six weeks in the future. That was standard. In the meantime, in physical therapy, I prepped my core muscles for surgery and a quick recovery. Unfortunately, bad instruction from a new tech in the PT office finished off the damaged disc. I could no longer walk without assistance. I waited. In a zero-gravity lawn chair in front of the big screen TV, I waited.

A few weeks later, the surgeon called. "I have an opening in a couple of hours, can you get up here?"

"Absolutely I can," I responded. Within hours, I was prepped and wheeled into surgery.

Waking in the hospital, I felt no pain. I was released the following morning, went down the street to Dr. Hahn's office, and was given instructions for recovery. Seeing him in the hallway, I walked easily over to give him a hug of gratitude. "I'll see you in two weeks," he responded, and sent me home to recover.

Two weeks later, I left his office with direct instructions: "Pick a race." Within four months, on Labor Day, I had a 5k under my belt. From that point forward, my training never slowed. The following summer, I concluded a season of sprint triathlons. The next season, I stepped into Olympic distance racing. While vacationing in San Diego, I decided to tackle the long distance race: 1.2 miles of swimming, 56 miles of biking, and finishing with a half marathon. Twelve weeks of training was left before the last opportunity of the year. I said "yes."

Six hours. That was the goal. In a little over two years, I moved from blinding pain and the inability to walk to being three months away from completing a Half-Ironman distance triathlon.

I was disciplined and never missed a training session. I wasn't so far removed from the pain that I clearly understood that the pain of pushing myself to perform would never be as bad as the pain I endured on Valentine's Day two years earlier.

An open water swim followed by 56 miles of rolling hills on a time trial bike, and a 13-mile run around north Oklahoma City, sent me across the finish line with the clock reading 6:00:50. Fifty fucking seconds. I missed my goal by fifty seconds. I celebrated with two weeks out of the pool, off the bike, and my shoes in the closet. Then started over again.

The pain of my previous injury put the temporary pain of training into perspective. Within three months, our family dealt with another experience that would make the discomfort of training not even worth mentioning. Training would be a relief.

2007 OKLAHOMA SOONERS
BIG 12 CHAMPIONS
11 - 3

HORRIFIC CELEBRATION

In December 2007, my maternal grandmother passed away. She had lived a glorious life and left us very peacefully with my mother by her side. Mason, my littlest one, and I would attend the funeral in Iowa. Summer was still an instructor at a ballet studio in Norman and the Christmas performance at the academy was coming up. She and my oldest would stay behind in town as Mason and I made the trip to Iowa.

This would be an opportunity to spend time with Mason that I didn't get very often. We were homeschooling her. Summer was an amazing teacher, and we had her reading at three years old. The two of them were very close. I was looking forward to some long overdue Dad time with her. We loaded the car with what the two of us would need for the few days we would be away and headed to Clarinda, Iowa to celebrate the life of my grandmother.

As we crossed the border from Kansas into Iowa, the landscape turned to the most beautiful pastures and fields, filled with three to four foot snowdrifts from the previous few days of snowfall. It was bright, shiny, and impactful enough to implant the images of the farming landscape at wintertime into my brain. There was enough ice in the tree branches to glisten and blind us as we drove the last few miles into town.

As I think back to the beginning of this trip, I can still picture this so clearly. I paid a lot of attention to what I was seeing during what might be one of my last trips into this geographical part of my history. My mother was born and raised close by in the tiny town of Yorktown, Iowa. She was the fourth of five children in a family where a consistent work ethic and a belief of work coming before play fostered tremendous success down the generational line. My grandparents modeled aspirational behavior and happiness every day of their lives. Each of my aunts and uncles was raised with the same opportunities. Varying degrees of success were experienced on that family tree, but regardless, all were happy in the lives they chose to lead. My maternal grandparents had done well.

My mother moved to Oklahoma to join her older sister, took a secretarial job at a well-respected law firm, and became active in the church. I looked at my mother's life as an example in politely accepting others' political differences and lifestyle choices, and withholding judgment. "Relationships over judgment," she would tell me. I understand her more every day. She is the wisest person I know.

One of my earliest memories as a child was my mother being very direct with me and telling me, "When you were very little, and I was holding you, God spoke to me very clearly: 'I have a plan for him.'" This was locked into my consciousness. I believed from the youngest age that I could do anything if it was part of that plan.

I would shortly discover the importance of my mother's foundational belief that we were part of an overarching plan, and the role of having vision in our lives, as the weekend turned into a nightmare for me and Mason.

We rolled into the snowpacked streets of Clarinda and found my aunt's home. She was the perfect living example of an Iowa farming wife, mother, and hostess. Her home would be the gathering place for the extended family as they returned to the region where so many of their stories began to unfold.

The funeral was a celebration of my grandmother's life. She was such a wonderful example of having created relationships that as we left the building, whispers of "what a life," "well done," and "I want that kind of service" were sprinkled through the conversations the rest of the day.

As we gathered back at my aunt's home in the evening, we filled our plates with Iowa farm comfort food. Closely-knit cousins that had grown up from childhood together could catch up on each other's lives while eating egg noodle soup loaded with fresh chicken. The family, which had gathered from all over the midwest, slowly left as the day came to a close, each heading back to one of two hotels in town before returning home.

Mason was dancing, entertaining, and giggling with members of the family that hadn't seen or been touched by her three-year-old joy when the weekend had begun. I got up from my chair for another serving of egg noodle soup. Ladling as many noodles into my bowl as I could, I leaned against the kitchen counter in conversation. As I caught up with my family, the most horrific screaming started coming from the living room.

I bolted in that direction. Mason had her hand to her face, covering her left eye, and was wailing uncontrollably. My cousin, who had been in the living room with her, attempted to comfort her as I tried to grasp what had just happened. She had lost her balance while playing and had fallen into the coffee table, taking a direct hit to her eye on the corner of the table. A one-in-a-million accident had just happened to my daughter.

I grabbed her and cradled her in my arms to get a look at the extent of her injury, pulling her hand away from her face. Her eye socket was horribly bruised already. I needed to see her eye. I pulled the lid back, and her eye appeared to be caved in on itself. No pupil or iris was visible, and the eye was blood red within minutes. I knew instantly that we needed to get care as soon as possible.

My sister accompanied me to the emergency room in the small town hospital. I sat in the passenger seat, cradling Mason, knowing a catastrophe had just occurred. The doctor on call attended to us right away. Looking into Mason's eye, he assured us that it had just incurred a deep bruise. I was in shock. I couldn't believe that the eye could take that kind of blow, especially given what I had seen, and only incur a deep bruise.

Well, as it turned out, it couldn't. The situation was much worse. But we didn't know that yet.

We packed immediately for home. I kept Summer, who was at home in Oklahoma, appraised of the situation at every opportunity. Mason had calmed down, and holding her eye, she cycled through sleeping and wakefulness as we made the seven-hour trip back to Oklahoma. I held out hope that because she had remained composed, her injury wasn't as bad as I thought. Arriving back in Norman, I took Mason immediately into an eye clinic by our neighborhood to get some answers. The doctor examined the eye, left the room, and returned to inform me that this was going to need further care by a specialist. He sent us into Oklahoma City to Children's Hospital. "They will be waiting for you," he told us.

I called Summer. "I'm coming to get you with Mason. It's bad, and we need to go to Children's. Be ready as soon as I drive up."

Shortly after we arrived at the facility and checked in, CAT scans were completed and the on-call resident made his observations. After consulting with his attending physician, he let us know that the damage was extensive. However, no further damage could occur at this point. We would need to arrive at the Dean McGee Eye Institute the following morning for follow up and a plan of action. She was three years old and now had one functioning eye.

We returned the next morning to receive an explanation of what had happened to the eye. It was disturbing, to say the least. The direct impact on her eye had ruptured the eye, blown the lens out, detached the retina, and caused the loss of vitreous fluid that fills the eye. The level of pain that accompanied the injury would debilitate adults, we were told. Mason had handled this like a champ. She would now become the poster child for eye trauma at the institute. For years following the accident, residents were brought in to review the case, observe the eye itself, and monitor the progress of her treatment.

We decided to begin a two-pronged approach that would benefit Mason the most in the long run. First, we would seek to save the eye itself. Things were happening daily in the field of eye medicine that had not been on the drawing board just five years before Mason's accident, and we wanted to give her every option to tap into those developments in the future. Secondly, we also needed to protect the healthy eye from accidental injury. She only had one left. Frames were fit to her face with lenses to protect both of her eyes. She would be in little frames for the foreseeable future.

A major surgery was scheduled for the physical reconstruction of her eye. It would allow for the eye to appear normal, and was the first option before anything more drastic would be considered for her cosmetically. Her primary physician for the treatment informed us that it would be a miracle if she had any useful vision from that eye in the future.

The level of support that we received from family and friends during this time was wonderful. The church we were involved with made sure we were fed. Cooking any meals beyond peanut butter and jelly or mac and cheese at home would have been next to impossible. We made it through the initial phase of Mason's trauma nutritionally sound thanks to the thoughtfulness of our church, family, and friends.

The surgery was an amazing example of a physician team working with talent, skill, and God's guidance to restore her left eye. The surgery was incredibly delicate. The eye was opened and her retina was "brushed" back into place, lining the inner walls of the eye itself—a masterful feat for the surgeon who was well-known in the field for this kind of intricate work. The vitreous fluid of the eye was replaced temporarily by an artificial fluid that was too thick to recycle. The fluid of the normal eye will typically recycle itself every twenty-four hours. We would let the eye recover and the fluid would be allowed to normalize. The final procedure is known as a "scleral buckle": a small band is put on or around the globe of the eye and tightened slightly to create a pressure to keep the retina pushed to the back of the eye. The goal was to regain a functioning eye that could track with her healthy right eye. The procedure took hours.

After a short recovery period, we were able to take Mason home and begin what would be years of therapy. We started by "patching" her good eye to force the injured eye to move with light and shadow recognition, and strengthen the muscles to track normally with the healthy eye. She would patch for up to five hours a day. A thick corrective lens was prescribed to maximize what the eye was capable of following the trauma. This was a chore for Summer and Mason over the next several years. Numerous checkups to document the pressure in the eye, adjust the corrective lens prescription, and replace the frames kept the three of us familiar to the staff of the institute for years.

I would meet the girls for these checkups when I was in town on appointment days. After the eye recovered from the trauma and the initial surgeries, these regular checkups became routine for the next couple of years. Mason had never slowed in her reading and education, however. On the way to the eye institute, she would read this scripture to us from the back seat of the car in the sweetest little girl's voice.

PSALM 102[A]

A prayer of an afflicted person who has grown weak and pours out a lament before the Lord.

1 Hear my prayer, Lord;
   let my cry for help come to you.
2 Do not hide your face from me
      when I am in distress.
      Turn your ear to me;
      when I call, answer me quickly.
3 For my days vanish like smoke;
      my bones burn like glowing embers.
4 My heart is blighted and withered like grass;
      I forget to eat my food.
5 In my distress I groan aloud
      and am reduced to skin and bones.

During this time period, some interesting developments started occurring. Mason was constantly getting prescription lens adjustments due to unexpected, but not unwelcome, changes in the eye. The changes had gotten to the point to where it was like we were on some kind of winning streak appointment after appointment, to see how many lines she could actually recognize on the eye chart with her corrected vision using only the damaged eye. After months of this routine, I sat in the dark room exam room as the doctor, his nurse, and Summer put Mason through this ordeal that she had become so accustomed to. "What does this line say?" Dr. Mike would ask. She nailed it. "What about this one?" She nailed it again. "And this?" She answered this correctly as well, starting to be amazed. With seemingly no consideration to the enormity of his observation, he said, "Mason, you could pass a driving test with that result."

The doctor, the nurse, Summer, and I were in shock. I recognized what that meant and said, "You told us it would be a miracle if she had any useful vision from that eye in the future." We sat in silence.

Dr. Mike responded, "Yes." We all burst into tears.

I had seen the damage to that child and her eye. For more than a year, I had seen an eye be knit back together from being crushed, and useful sight return to it. We all had.

My back injury and the recovery that followed was on one level. I could explain that away with a solid training plan, discipline, and fortitude. This eye accident and what I witnessed was a next-level interaction. I had known for years that God was engaged with us on a personal level, and now I was blessed to see it firsthand.

1 Hear my prayer, Lord;
    let my cry for help come to you.
2 Do not hide your face from me
      when I am in distress.
      Turn your ear to me;
      when I call, answer me quickly.

TWO-WHEELED AGGIES

I trained like a beast in 2008 for one race, the same Half-Ironman distance race that I had raced the previous year, missing my personal goal by fifty seconds. My goal was to try again to beat the six-hour mark. My training was stress relief following Mason's eye injury. I never missed a workout leading up to the race.

I finished in 5:40, over twenty minutes faster than my previous attempt. I had accomplished what I set out to do: finish a long-distance triathlon in under six hours. It was respectable achievement for somebody with a family and career.

I never competed in triathlon again. I hung up my bike, continuing to look at it as a screensaver. It was a beautiful red, black, and white Cervelo P2 Carbon. I rode it on a few more training rides to stay in some aerobic shape, but was thrilled to eventually give it to a younger cousin to ride in her first triathlon.

Although I've stopped cycling, I've never stopped running. I find the solitude a wonderful time to be alone in my thoughts. My legs still feel young, and it was always my best leg of the three, probably due to being the one I started later in life.

With the time previously dedicated to training for triathlon, Summer and I devoted more time together to building our wealth. Following the housing crisis of 2008, we invested more in nontraditional assets, and in ourselves. We attacked our mortgage with a vengeance. I followed what was happening in the the precious metals market and real estate. I invested objectively and with nice returns once I realized that the state of American politics was an absolute joke. The politics of division kept people separated to be mobilized for use at election times. My willingness to listen to my higher self took a huge leap forward when I turned off the talking heads and began thinking for myself.

Summer had buried herself into Mason's homeschooling while I immersed myself into the sustainability of not only our financial assets but a way of life that was based on good principles of living. Mason's eye continued to recover and her injury never held her back from achieving an amazing homeschooled classical education. That process was one of the best decisions we made.

I found it fascinating to follow what people were designing in the agriculture sphere. Using specific design principles, parts of the world where owning any quantity of land larger than a postage stamp was unthinkable delivered impressive results. The joy of working in their own backyards to produce most of what was on the dining room table every night was tangible.

Growing a little of our own food was enriching, if for nothing other than the feeling of producing something of value. With a few weekends invested in building out areas to plant little crops of our favorite vegetables on our quarter acre lot in Norman, we were soon impressive backyard producers ourselves. Okra, zucchini, green beans, watermelons, and eggplants decorated the kitchen. The spicy peppers made up the base of many salsas we consumed. This was my new, next pursuit. I began my education in sustainable agriculture design and I wanted to go bigger.

Permaculture is an approach to designing property based on flourishing natural ecosystems. The elements of the design are organized based on the frequency of human interaction with the plants or animals. The home is at the center, with elements requiring less care further away. Many of the characteristics associated with this approach are familiar to most people: mulching, rainwater collection, composting, and raised-bed gardening are basic principles of permaculture. Free-range chickens and the rotational grazing of cattle are examples of how animals can be incorporated on a larger scale.

We learned the principles of the method in short order. Implementing them successfully was the challenge. But my mind systemized the process fairly quickly. Much like my success in the pharmaceutical industry and the sport of triathlon, I found a way that worked for me and Summer to implement the methods, harvest, and enjoy the fruits of our labor.

Meanwhile, my career rocked along. A tremendous reduction in the sales force had taken place over the last several years. Multiple divisions that had up to 12,000 employees at one time had slowly been reduced by 80 percent. Yet I had remained a fixture in the Oklahoma City medical community and proceeded to move through the fields of urology, psychiatry, and into the women's health division. I was extremely relaxed as a man working in a division where the different compounds I represented were all one form or another of hormone replacement therapy. The time spent here was invaluable to me later, when the knowledge of HRT and the benefit-to-risk data would become much more personal.

Our investments were doing well, despite not following the script to stay in the market and trust it always goes up. The precious metals market was performing, as was our enjoyment of being outside and cultivating something of value. But somehow, I just couldn't relax. Something was missing.

As we drove to Chicago for a week-long getaway, a vehicle pulling a trailer loaded with a Harley-Davidson motorcycle passed us. I looked at that and a light went off in my head. "Wouldn't that be fun to ride on the weekends and make day trips to our favorite places to eat around the state?" I asked. I don't even remember what Summer said in response. But it wasn't "no." And if it wasn't no, that meant full steam ahead.

I had ridden motorcycles from the time I was five years old. Long-time friends of my parents had minibikes for the kids, and I would ride in the undeveloped land of future subdivisions in Oklahoma City. The bulldozed hills were perfect. Unsupervised training on little 50cc motorcycles and Mom's instructions of "let me know who you are with" and "be home for dinner" were my tickets to being very comfortable at an early age. My father brought home a street bike that I rode in high school, and I later graduated into a larger sport bike as my main form of transportation when I was enrolled and living in the fraternity at OU. I eventually sold that bike for a woman.

Within weeks of returning from Chicago I had that 2013 Harley-Davidson Street Glide, matte black finish, in the garage. I hadn't been on a bike in twenty-five years. It was amazingly powerful, and heavy for me at 150 pounds. However, within days, I was as relaxed as the last day I rode my last bike. Thinking back to how much fun I had learning to ride as a little boy gave me the brilliant idea of encouraging that for my girls. A scooter each for Summer and our oldest daughter, and a 50cc minibike for Mason. She was eight. Of course, I needed a 250cc motocross bike for the trails I would ride alongside her.

The scooters never did get ridden very much. Our oldest never put the time into feeling secure on hers. She was in her first year at OU and her car was her primary mode of transportation. Summer's desire to ride the scooter far exceeded her ability to find the time to make it happen. Mason was a different story. She rode the minibike around the front and back yards with no fear, and training wheels. Yes, I mounted training wheels on a little dirt bike for my daughter that could hit 40 mph. Now, if Mason was getting comfortable, and I was comfortable, I couldn't have Summer feeling left out. A new Honda 125cc would be just perfect for her.

Alas, a memorable trip to the motorcycle trails and courses in east Oklahoma City turned into a fiasco.

Two of the worst decisions I have made with my beautiful wife of over twenty-one years are making that dirt bike purchase and following it up with being the person who attempted to instruct her on how to ride a motorcycle. That is a huge statement, because this list includes what comes later! Pants, jersey, neck protection, knee and elbow pads, plus the coolest helmet for a woman at the bike park didn't survive entry into the trail section. In peak alpha male mode, I was trying to explain that balancing the right-hand throttle and front brake, left-hand clutch, left foot gear shifting, and right foot rear brake should be easy. Trying to navigate the handlebars of a 125cc motocross bike between the two steel posts and remain balanced *was* easy. An easy way to eject a thirty-six-year-old wife and mother off the back of the bike and into divorce court! Fortunately for me, she had an awesome attitude about the experience. (We were all about experiences, right?) I never pushed the motorcycle experience again.

While we were having motorcycle adventures, I had been continuing to learn all I could about the principles of designing properties for sustainability. Meanwhile, sections of our neighborhood had been shifting, to put it nicely, for the last few years. Kids would roam the streets in the hours after midnight, unlocked cars would be robbed of contents, and garage doors couldn't be left up for any length of time if one wanted to avoid losing one's valuables. We experienced all of the same incidents ourselves. I had had it. I hate that shit. I worked hard for my stuff. We were outta there.

Summer and I belatedly celebrated our tenth wedding anniversary in Santa Fe, New Mexico, where we had honeymooned. Our times away from home always gave us time to assess how we were spending our lives. On this trip, the time together in the car and as we celebrated our marriage led to another experience. We decided to leave Norman and search for a small homestead outside of town. Ten to fifteen acres would be just the right amount for us. It would fit into our budget and give us room to grow into new experiences that had to burst forth. We also wanted to be close enough that our families could enjoy rural life with us.

We found a place rather quickly. I'm decisive and like to make things happen that take other people years to get around to doing. The property, twenty minutes from our home in Norman, was between thirteen and fourteen acres—three acres surrounding the house and eleven acres of pasture. I had been past it on training rides while prepping for triathlon. It would be a few minutes further for my parents to visit us, and a bit closer for Summer's. We were moved into the property within two months.

Moving from a well-designed home in the city of Norman with dependable utilities to rural country life with rural electricity and propane tanks for heating was an adjustment. Of course, we needed a new four-wheel drive Toyota Tundra for our new homestead. Summer took possession of the truck and loved it. We traded Summer's motorcycle in for a large Honda ATV that could readily move things for us when we didn't need the new truck. The ATV was her baby. Mason upgraded her minibike to a Sport ATV. We purchased a large zero-turn mower on the research and advice of a good friend and my future manager at the company. The mower could cut a tremendous amount of lawn fast. We shared the mowing responsibility between us. We have fond memories of cutting four-foot-high wild grasses down for trails so we could ride through our eleven acres of pasture.

***

On the afternoon of May 13, 2013, a category F5 tornado ravaged Moore, Oklahoma. We were thirty miles from Moore. Driving home, watching the storm from the south edge, I arrived back at the ranch to find Summer already had us prepped and using the generator and backup battery systems I'd designed several years before and brought with us to the country.

Storms raged all night and our area was devastated by 100 mph wind and hail. Storm winds in Moore peaking at 210 mph killed twenty-four and injured two hundred and twelve. We awoke in the morning to find every roof on our property needing replacement. The stable, storage building, well-house, and the 1600-square-foot building that housed the gym, truck, and small vehicles all needed totally new roofs. We had been in our home for less than a month. Our upstairs windows were gone, and that roof was totaled as well.

It would take over a year to recover. I couldn't do the property reconstruction, but I could design what the whole property could be like moving forward.

I had some *home* work.

2013 OKLAHOMA SOONERS

SUGAR BOWL CHAMPIONS

11 - 2

THE ARK

We had purchased the property in Noble fully intending to design a homestead that could produce for us. We knew it would be difficult, and were fully aware that our time and labor would be heavily invested in the property. The damaged buildings would take time to repair, but that was simply a logistical problem due to the availability of labor and material following a storm that had killed dozens.

I received my Permaculture Design Certificate (PDC) using the property as the basis for my final submission. My project focused on the design implementation of our plant, animal, and water systems. It took tremendous amounts of research, but in Oklahoma, gathering the data wasn't as difficult as one might believe. I had to gather information on wind patterns, primarily the prevailing wind patterns and solar exposures at different times of the year, as well as topographical maps of the land for water flow purposes and buried pipeline maps.

While I was the one getting the education, gathering data, and building the presentation for submission, Summer and Mason were giddy about the prospects of gathering an assortment of critters to house on the ranch. We all went to work doing our thing. The property was a blank slate. Our families were fully behind us as we began to develop the property.

Summer's father is an amazing backyard gardener, spending almost every waking hour working with his own little oasis in the middle of Norman. He enjoyed seeing what his daughter was investing her energy into those first few years. Seeing the two connect with the common interest was lovely. Had he chosen to do something on a bigger scale that didn't require the daily time and attention, he always had an area available for him. My mother, having grown up in Iowa, was very familiar with agriculture, the animals, and the effect of weather. My dad was thrilled about the opportunity to live vicariously through our experiences. For years, I had heard him say "I wish…" He was fascinated as I kept him informed of exactly what I was implementing and the methodology behind it. The placement and the pattern of every system had a reason, usually more than one. Mine was a holistic design. And beyond my dad, I was always willing to bore our visitors with a lecture on the "deeper why" of the design. I couldn't hire any locals to help with heavy equipment. They just couldn't see the vision I had for the property. We would do it all manually.

An orchard was planted behind our home, laid out in a half moon pattern, with alternating varieties of apple, peach, apricot, pear, and plum trees. This method made it difficult for pests to gain an advantage because each tree has unique characteristics that don't always appeal to the same insects.

Summer and I made multiple trips to Texas together, gathering the right varieties of trees, and sometimes multiple varieties of the same fruit producers. We had a planting party on the property. We invited family, friends, and friends of family to dig holes to the correct depth, plant trees, and vest themselves in the success of our endeavor. Between each tree, we planted some really interesting, hard to find plants, in addition to a variety of roses. Native locust trees were interspersed within the orchard, all of this working together to make it difficult for fruit-loving insects to gain advantage, and creating a favorable space for the predatory insects to manage the rest. At least that was the idea.

The Oklahoma forestry department has a program every fall that encourages the planting of trees and vegetation native to the state. An incredible variety of trees and shrubbery, including native fruit-producing trees favorable to wildlife, were available for purchase. The unit price dropped significantly as the quantity purchased increased. I ordered an assortment of five hundred individual seedlings. Vitex shrubbery, loblolly pine, Oklahoma redbuds, pin oak trees, and a variety of native shrubbery arrived in bundles of fifty. For months, Summer and I kept the seedlings moist as we planted day after day, after work and on the weekends. We created a row of beautiful loblolly pines and Vitex that would block the view of our home from the road on the east side of the property, and lined each side of the three hundred foot drive with redbud trees. None of it obstructed our views of our pasture, our neighbor's home, or the beautiful sunsets on a nightly basis.

As mentioned, Summer and Mason were excited about the possibility of raising chickens and gathering eggs. The two had done their research on what breeds of chickens we would raise and ordering from a catalog, chose our flock based on egg production, heartiness, and beauty. Over a dozen newly-hatched chicks arrived within two days. Learning how to feed, water, and care for our future flock was the girls' responsibility. One yellow chick was a rooster that proved to be a favorite. We named him Daisy (should've been a clue of what was to come), and he grew into a beautiful specimen of rooster. Prettier than any other chicken on the ranch. Roosters can be unpredictable and mean, particularly to children. But Daisy was gentle with Mason as she would feed, water, and gather eggs.

Hawks were a constant threat to the flock. Sweeping down from above on an unsuspecting hen, a hawk could consume a chicken in minutes. The talons on a rooster, while not like a hawk's, were significant, and a deterrent. Daisy would perch himself to protect the chickens in full view of the raptors. He did his job well for a number of years. When he became sick and passed away, we were horribly saddened by the loss. Daisy was the only chicken we buried during our time on the ranch.

We ordered over three dozen more chicks, increasing the total to over four dozen. Hawk and coyote incursions cost us over the years, as did the brutally cold winters, but we maintained a consistent flow of eggs during our years on the ranch. We moved the chickens around the property every week or two in a mobile chicken coop that I designed and built on the base of a two-wheeled utility trailer. We used our four-wheeler to pull it wherever we wanted our chickens ranging on the property. They would eat bugs in the vegetation, fertilize the ground for future growth, and rotate to the next area. As we moved the chickens, the productivity that followed behind them was amazing evidence of how well the system worked.

We purchased guinea fowl and housed them in an enclosure that my dad and I finished in a day's work. The guineas were funny creatures with a funny sound, always traveling in a small, tight flock. They are wild and native to Oklahoma. They can, however, identify one place as "home." We released them in the mornings and closed them up each night before dark. They ravaged the tick population around the house, much to our relief and the dogs'. Unfortunately, with their native independent nature, the guinea fowl didn't last long. Predators swiftly took their toll.

One of my colleagues who lived in Arkansas raised rabbits as pets. Earning the well-deserved reputation of productivity, one of her rabbits delivered more babies than my colleague could possibly handle. She inquired if Mason would adopt, and after receiving a quick affirmative answer. she brought them to a company meeting. I kept the babies in the hotel bathtub for several days before returning home. Mason would begin some of her finest work with those animals.

I designed a large moveable hutch for the rabbits. The four wheels were removable, allowing the hutch to nest on the ground. The flooring was a series of slats, not solid. The rabbits would consume the grass between the slats, fertilizing for new growth along the way, and like the chickens, would be moved periodically around the property. The first hutch, built by my father could house all four rabbits. With the potential for the rabbits to proliferate, though, we produced a smaller version for one rabbit each that could be moved like a wheelbarrow, with two wheels on the front and handles on the back. My father did a masterful job building these as well. We never had a rabbit escape, and coyotes were never successful getting to any of them. Mason cared for those rabbits all of the years at the ranch, showing them at the county fair, winning ribbons, and later bringing her favorites with us to the city and our HOA.

The dogs were family and lived in the house with us. Sam, a small shepherd-mix rescue, came with us from Norman. My oldest daughter had found him. He'd lived for more than a year of his life in a two-foot by two-foot cage. At the ranch, he blossomed. He became attached to me and never left my side once I got home from work. Not being allowed into the pasture, he would watch our every move from the porch. He also loved to sit in the middle of the long drive as if he was the guardian, but that job belonged to Bullet. A large German shepherd, acquired and raised from a puppy, Bullet protected us, the home, and everything within the perimeter of our fences. He was a fixture on the ranch, known by the neighbors and the delivery drivers. To strangers, he was an imposing threat. He did his job well.

Two Pomeranians, Kona and Khaki, also came with us from Norman. They were dumb as rocks. They proved the point that one should never buy two puppies at the same time. It was hard to discipline either one, never knowing who the offender was when we left them by themselves. They were sweet, though, stayed out of the way, and were watched over by Bullet when they were outside.

We submitted the design of the property to Geoff Lawton, an Australian consultant, designer, teacher, and speaker. He is a worldwide expert, with clients that include private individuals, governments, NGOs, and multinational corporations. He awarded me my permaculture certification based on the design of the property.

We implemented the planned systems with varying degrees of success. The native species that we planted flourished, as intended. But we were constantly reminded over the course of the seven years that Mother Nature can be a real bitch—not including the storm damage we incurred within the first month.

Torrential rain washed out half our fruit trees in Year One. We successfully replaced the losses and were met the following year with 100 days straight of temperatures topping 100 degrees Fahrenheit. It was amazing anything survived. Summer, Mason, and I ventured out to feed and water the livestock and trees, then scurried back to the air conditioning as quickly as we could. Chickens are tough in the hot and cold weather, especially if given a bit of warmth on the coldest nights, and our flock made it through.

I was driving myself into the ground to make the ranch successful. But successful at what? This was not a ranch that would sustain our lifestyle by itself. It was giving us some pretty cool experiences. But where were all the experiences leading me?

I couldn't stand still. Within the first two years, I had implemented every aspect of the design, but one. I had eleven acres of pasture that needed maintaining. I could maintain it by purchasing expensive equipment, hiring it done, or following through and completing the design project … with cattle.

I wanted to graze cattle on our small acreage, and I had no experience.

2014 OKLAHOMA SOONERS

8 - 5

BEDDY

Summer and I were working to repair the fences, mowing, and trimming the property when our neighbors to the north, David and Shayna, stopped by for a visit. We sat on the side of the road, enthralled with each other. David and Shayna were the Ingalls (*Little House* type neighbors) of Noble, Oklahoma. The best neighbors one could hope to have next door. Even if next door was a quarter mile and two pastures away. Standing by the road, listening to each other's backgrounds, we clicked. Despite life experiences that were worlds apart, we would grow to trust and rely on each other for the years we both were on our properties. David, a diesel mechanic by trade, knew something about everything to do with home and country living. My life experiences offered little when it came time for engine, plumbing, or home repairs. But I did have another pair of hands and the willingness to put them to use. We would develop a great relationship over the next six years. Neither of us hesitated to ask for help when needed. What a gift they were to us.

As we crouched by the cars that first day, saying our goodbyes through the window, I mentioned that I wanted to run some cattle on our place, and David's face lit up! He had around fifty head of Black Angus cattle that we loved watching graze from our wrap-around porch in the evenings and weekends. He said, "Then I'm going to get you started with your first cow as a housewarming gift!"

That is a helluva gift. As we found out later, immersing ourselves into the cattle during our time on the ranch, an expensive and valuable one. And unexpected, to say the least. We stayed by the side of the road for a little while longer, then said our goodbyes.

We could see each other's homes and properties from our windows and porches. It was a huge comfort and sense of security for all of us. We were there for each other if the need arose. When homes are a quarter of a mile apart, a clear view of our neighbor's home was a bonus, for personal space as well as safety. Both pieces of land were pleasant to gaze over in the evening.

Helping David to load and move cattle from one of his properties to another, delivering basic healthcare to the herd one at a time, and setting fence posts was righteous work. I received such an education and joy in helping him accomplish things whenever he asked for help. And he never failed to be there when I needed him, too. David seemed to know something about everything, he loved teaching, and was one of the wisest men I've known. He was fifteen years younger and seemed like my grandpa.

Several months later, in November, I was working out in the gym. Our gym was a 1600-square-foot steel building that the previous owner had built for his hobbies and projects. I had taken half of it and put in all the things that I felt were necessary to continue the kind of workouts I had done since I was a sixteen-year-old: padded floors, squat racks, benches, free weights, a treadmill, and a barre for Summer's ballet workouts and stretching. It was getting cold as the sun set in the late afternoon when David walked in, startling me. This wasn't normal, because typically we had warning of someone being on the property. The dogs would bark or the sound of vehicles coming up the gravel drive would give some hint of visitors. But the dogs loved David.

We could go weeks without visiting. If one of us showed up at the other's place, it was usually important. Smiling, he exclaimed, "If you're not busy, I've got your housewarming gift! Let's go pick her out!"

We were starting our cattle grazing experience spontaneously on a cold November night. I'm not sure who was more excited, him or me. "Absolutely!" I responded.

I hustled back into the main house, to change from my workout clothing into jeans, boots, and my Carhartt jacket. I definitely needed something a little warmer than workout tights. On the ranch, I had learned that working into the evening out in the open pasture could get damn cold. I went into the house hollering for Summer and Mason.

In the country, if you came in excited, it was important and one better be quick to differentiate between good news and bad news. It could be anything from animal emergencies, water well malfunctions, or spreading the joy of one of the many accomplishments that we had over the years. "David's here! We are getting our cow tonight!" I exclaimed. They moved into high gear, asking what they needed to do to get us ready at home. Looking back, it was a huge milestone in the experience of our living on the ranch.

David knew firsthand the joy of giving and doing for others. Pleasant as usual, he invited me to jump in his small white pickup and we headed to his place. We went through multiple gates into the pasture, hooked up the livestock trailer, and went to review the animals. He was letting me pick our own from some he had set aside as good options.

It was a large number of cattle to look over for someone doing it for the first time. Also, it was getting dark fast. The headlights, along with the lights from the house over the corral, made the job of choosing easier. We quickly narrowed the number to two, based on demeanor and age. David was letting me choose, but knowing that I had no experience to work from, he hinted, "I been watching these two, and they got real good natures about them." I smiled, thinking now "we" were making some headway. He continued, "This one shows lots of patience with the calves in the group. She'll likely be a good momma."

Well, that was a good sign. "Okay, let's go—" I began.

He cut me off. "But you know I think this other one has some good qualities..." He trailed off his sentence. I wanted to hear all of his thoughts. They were both big two-year-olds, and it would be hard to choose between the two for our first.

"Let's go with the one that has the nice demeanor. We want calves, and Mason is small and she will be doing the work with me."

David agreed. "You're right! That's a great choice!"

I watched as he started the process of separating the chosen from the others. They were all Black Angus cattle and it was dark—quite the task. It was like a game for him, frustratingly fun, with a clearly defined winner at the end of the contest. In the future, I was always drawn to this part of the process: the time for the separation of the animals. It was a competition with fifteen hundred pounds of animal moving fast. The adrenaline would spike because you could get hurt, and badly, if you weren't careful. The whole process captivated me.

Using the truck lights and the lights over the corral, we separated the chosen cow from the others and sent her down the lane between the fences and up the ramp into the back of the trailer. She always loaded easy from that time on, whenever it was time to travel. We had nothing for her in the way of supplies. But David did. He threw a feeding trough into the bed of the truck that would last us all the years we were there at the ranch. He added mineral blocks and protein cubes to all the supplies one uses or picks up for a day's work with the cattle. We hauled her back through the gates, down the drive, and over onto our property. Summer and Mason were so excited seeing us turn into our gravel drive, carefully pulling the trailer to the stable and loading gate. This was a big event for the three of us. Having all grown up in the city, it was a blessing to have been gifted an animal that would provide us a start to such a new experience. She unloaded as easily as she loaded. We kept her corralled for a couple of days, to give us some time to check the perimeter fences for any gaps. The cattle will find them, as we learned later with some other heifers we added to the group. David left us soon after the drop off. It was dark and cold. What an evening. There were no lights at our stable for us to continue, so we went to the house. We were cattle ranchers now. With a herd of one.

Our work was just beginning. As the years went on, the importance of that evening and what it did for our family can't be overstated. David and Shayna were angels.

We accepted the routines, chores, and responsibilities for the care of not only the cattle, but of every other animal on the property as the new normal. To put it simply, if we didn't do work that needed to be done, our animals died.

Summer and Mason named the new addition Beddy. It was the safe thing to do if one wanted to ensure she didn't end up on a dinner plate anytime in the near future. She was as gentle as we hoped she would be when we chose her to bring home. Mason was responsible for keeping the cattle trough filled with water and we loved bringing her back to the stable from the pasture with a shake of the bucket containing protein cubes. All the cattle loved those as a treat. We could get them to do almost anything for us with protein cubes as an incentive.

Months later, we decided to add more cattle. With our property on the small side at under fifteen acres, if I wanted to maximize the number of animals we could graze and keep them healthy, I would need to be very efficient. With my previous certification in permaculture design, I understood that I would be serving the cattle dinner daily, instead of them having the whole pasture as a buffet.

***

I found a man who would teach me a little more than the basics. I already knew what to do, but I needed to learn the actual physical process of implementing the system. I wanted to know the most efficient equipment to use and how to use it. Greg Judy, an international expert in rotational cattle grazing, was going to be teaching a three-day class on the technique in North Carolina. It was a class for beginners. Absolutely no experience was required. If you had experience, you were not a candidate. I was accepted upon payment and was excited to attend.

Within weeks, at my "real job," the company announced another complete restructure of the sales force. I promptly coordinated a return to the cardiology division to work with a previous manager and started the training process for certification on anticoagulation and the usage of a fairly new compound. The process would overlap with my grazing course. I received the training outline and saw that I had three days between sessions on anticoagulation. They were the three days I would be in North Carolina.

I drove the Tundra across the country. Arriving early on the first day of grazing class, I immediately began taking notes and formulating questions I wouldn't have a chance to ask this easily again. The training was hosted by an emergency room physician familiar with the new medication I would be representing to the medical community. We hit it off immediately. Both small homesteaders working in healthcare, we could compare notes and laugh about the new experiences we constantly put our families through year after year.

I learned that an electric line with a power source, posts that held the line to limit and mark boundaries, and discipline to change the grazing area daily was all one needed to get started. Hands-on activities of reeling the line in and out, plus information on water sourcing methods and financial saving tips finished the course. I drove cross-country back to Oklahoma the night after class ended. The following day, I certified on the new anticoagulant and its proper approved usage.

In four days, I had become a certified rotational grazing specialist working in cardiology with a focus on Black Angus cattle and DVT treatment.

***

I decided to move the cattle in a structured pattern onto different pieces of pasture daily. They'd graze everything in that assigned area, head down, for twenty-four hours, eating and pressing the rest into the soil behind them. The pattern presses the manure and stubble into the ground to come up again with lush growth we'd graze again three to four months later as the herd rotated back to the area. The process can be used with herds of one to herds that number in the thousands. In Oklahoma, this method was not widely used because of the availability of land for cattle. Efficiency wasn't necessarily a top priority for everyone. But with a small homestead and a desire to graze cattle without losing money, I would need do something a bit different if I wanted more than a couple of cows.

Molly was the second addition. Multiple calves followed. One of the new additions was awful, always wanting what was on the other side of the fence. We had to cut and repair our fence multiple times in returning her to our pasture. One early Monday morning proved a case in point.

Summer and Mason left for errands to Norman, and slowed for a cow in the road. It was Lucy, half a mile from home. Mason retrieved a bucket of cubes and lured the heifer all the way back to our land. After that, Mason and I took her to market within days. A registered Black Angus, she was intended to give us multiple calves for a number of years. But there was no way I was risking anyone's safety for that damn cow.

2015 OKLAHOMA SOONERS
BIG 12 CHAMPIONS
11 - 2

SUPERHEROES AND SECRET IDENTITIES

Within two years, we had increased our little group of cattle to seven, maxing out what we could do with rotational grazing without the costly supplementing of feed. That would've defeated the purpose of what were doing every day. Mason and I moved those cattle after I came home from work and worked out. We would call the cattle in with the shake of the cube bucket. As they licked the trough clean, Mason and I would race to the pasture and rewire the next section. They loved moving onto the fresh grass as much as they liked those cubes, so we were on a timer.

We took great pride in the success of the grazing. It was easy to see the environmental benefit of raising cattle this way. The effect on the pasture saved us from purchasing tractors to mow it or from having to hire someone to maintain it for us. Financially, the cattle paid for themselves. The cost of cubes and supplemental hay in the winter were covered by revenue of taking one animal to market.

The homestead was a smooth operation. We had an efficient routine between the three of us to make sure everything was maintained. Summer gathered eggs and let the chickens out in the morning. Chickens were delivering a dozen eggs daily. Mason continued the watering of the animals throughout the day. Whatever they needed, she gave them, several times daily in the summer or breaking ice in the winter. At thirteen, she was busting ass, and was fully vested in the place.

The daily routine with the animals and sustaining the organic growth of the property itself on the weekends was a massive commitment of time. Maintaining the trees we planted, both native from the Forest Service and the fruit trees in our small orchard, left us little time for traveling or being away from our home more than the day. And never overnight. A north and east facing covered porch that wrapped around the front of our home was decked out with rocking chairs and had us recovered by the end of most days, the exceptions being in the coldest parts of winter.

Our parents loved visiting when they could. Within an hour's drive, they could leave the city and experience the silence of the countryside. It was an escape for our loved ones. Escape from lives where they found it difficult to say "no" to babysitting grandchildren, children's activities, or demanding work schedules and doctor appointments. I found the fifty-minute drive home every day an excellent way to decompress after a day in the medical field.

I was shedding my cares and concerns like leaves off a tree. The girls were self-sufficient. The oldest was now engaged. Summer continued to use her gift of teaching for Mason's education. My career was at a high point. I was successful and getting better as my relationships grew stronger. There was no danger of me losing my job; I was a valued member of a high-performing team. The mortgage on the ranch had been paid off and my relationship with Summer was solid. Without the burdens that weigh on the minds of so many in our culture, burdens smothering any recognition of one's deepest desires, I started listening.

As I drove home decompressing one evening, it wasn't hard to hear the voice inside my head expressing gratitude for not only the life, but the wife I had been given. *It has been a long time. There is no one that loves you more than she does. Finish the job. Get to know each other.*

I heard it. I wanted Summer to know how much she meant to me. Many women struggle for that knowledge after the pursuit is over and some form of partnership is established.

I asked my parents to host our daughter for a weekend while we reignited a relationship long set on "simmer." They were pleased to be grandparents for a few days. I had Summer clear her schedule for the weekend, and prepare for a few days of being taken care of, as if she was starting the dating process all over again. I didn't say much about my plans, but I was clear that there would never be a safer time to reveal each other's shadows more than now. We weren't leaving each other. It would be safe. And exciting.

The plan was a marriage renewal weekend for two, organized with a purpose of increasing the knowledge of each other's pasts. Over the weekend, we would ask questions designed to give us a better understanding of each other and build more security in the relationship for the future. We answered questions about old relationships, clearing the air of stories we'd told ourselves about the other. Filling the empty spaces with truth. Cementing the real stories as we would move forward together. Sex and margaritas were abundant. We asked for what we wanted from the other and found it safe and exciting to get it.

What we weren't expecting was how much laughter we would experience. Dropping our guards, we pulled off one of the funniest experiences of our marriage. I had purchased some items from the party store for a skit that we would act out as part of the weekend. I handed her a gift sack with her items, an instruction card, and I took mine. "I'll meet you back in the living room when you're ready," I said. Summer left for the bedroom.

Opening her sack to find a sword, a shield emblazoned with "WW," and a crown for an Amazonian princess, she went into character of Diana Prince, Wonder Woman. She pulled the card from the sack. It read "Seduce Batman." Sauntering out into the living room to find me in the Dark Knight's mask, she started making conversation. "What's up, Bruce?"

"Fighting crime, Diana," I stoically responded.

"I'm lonely," she said.

"Where's Robin?" I asked, watching my Bat-computers.

We couldn't go on. We were laughing so hard at each other wearing children's costume accessories. Summer held a sword, a shield, and wore a crown. I could not see out of the black hooded mask because the tears of laughter were flowing, blinding me and ruining my ability to continue.

We ended that evening to retire to the bedroom. The next morning, we slept late. I darted out barely dressed to let the chickens out and water the cattle, then hustled back to the house and jumped back in bed.

"I want to get a tattoo," Summer told me, seemingly out of nowhere. This was not an easy "yes" for me. "My sisters and I have talked about getting matching tattoos," she explained. Gulp.

I responded quickly, "I'll get one with you." That was decided.

Later, I talked to Summer about something I wanted her to consider.

Before Summer and I got married, I'd visited about the relationship with a wise counselor who knew my history and my personality. With there being thirteen years between us, and her being young when we married, it would behoove us to allow for her growth in life experience. The words of advice were invaluable to me, and I thought back to them now. "I would like you to consider taking more of a decisive leadership role here at home," I stated. I had my career, the property, the cattle, and our future; I was responsible for everything. "You are wonderful at what you do. You make great decisions, and everything you've done as a wife and a mother, you've been successful at."

There is not much better than knowing you have the faith, trust, and respect of the person you love the most. She ran with this request.

We ended our weekend together. We met our daughter and my parents for lunch, and they noticed the increased bonding between us.

***

Within weeks, I had taken the lead on finding just the right tattoo artist. Summer took more responsibility at home while my career flourished. Letting go of my need to control everything in my life was a gift. Summer's role in our relationship expanded while I was making room for something else unknown at the time.

I found an amazing tattoo artist in Oklahoma City, a female artist originally from Wisconsin, and began a journey with her that was totally unexpected. In saying "yes" to the body art, we gave ourselves an experience of a lifetime. Steph Brandl led us on incredible trip that didn't stop with the initial ropes around our right ankles. We became consumed with the experience of sitting in the chair. The shop, the artists, the honesty, were all an experience that would imprint into our lives in addition to our skin.

After tattooing the ropes, we memorialized the seduction. Steph tattooed the Wonder Woman logo on Summer's left hip and inked the Bat on the upper left side of my chest. For over two years, we alternated sitting in Steph's chair while the other sat in support. Every three weeks, we spent our Friday afternoons with the roughest, toughest, kindest souls in Oklahoma City's world of body art. I told Summer how much I loved the people at the shop, Steph, Tweety, Tober, Jess, James, and Jimmy. They were our crew. We spent over two years with them.

Summer followed Wonder Woman with a right arm sleeve beautifully inked with her father's Native American artwork. A ballerina highlighted a back piece, with a snake wrapping her hips to flow into stems of roses down the right leg. We both wore the image of a quail on our left wrist, an image taken from a six hundred year old piece of pottery found when ground was broken for the El Dorado Hotel in Santa Fe where we had honeymooned.

My right arm contained Scripture from John 18:37 and John 10:9, testifying to Jesus being exactly who he said he was. The passages were scripted on the lower and upper arm, respectively. My right forearm was wrapped in roses, with my upper arm wearing an amazing piece of artwork that had been commissioned years before I met Steph. The buyer never returned to have it inked. She offered it to me and I readily accepted. A stairway to heaven with a gate opening at the top wrapped around my bicep, tricep, and shoulder.

We weren't close to being finished.

The following winter, Summer slipped in the mud around the chicken coop, severely herniating a disc in her back. She spent much of the year in recovery. Sessions of physical therapy gave her temporary relief; steroid injections into her lower back offered slightly longer periods of comfort. Our family physician finally discovered that Summer's sacroiliac (SI) joints had been misaligned with the slip in the mud, and keeping those in alignment brought a more lasting relief. Then, a surprising shoulder injury required a major surgery and rehabilitation to finish Summer's year. Still, we continued to sit in the chair.

***

My request for my wife to take more of a decisive role in our home signaled that what had been an internal struggle was now manifesting externally. I was incredibly comfortable with my masculinity. Who I was as a man, husband, father, and son was reflected every day in my life, career, and relationships. My wardrobe reflected this, for my life on the ranch and as well as in my professional life as a healthcare specialist. Now, things started to change in my fashion. I started to wear a slimmer, more feminine pant that rode higher on the ankle. I placed more pastels in my closet, hanging them next to the ties that were once an absolute standard in the industry, now undisturbed. When asked about my change in style, I referenced Russell Westbrook's fashion sense. A fixture at the time with the NBA's Oklahoma City Thunder, Westbrook was known for his trendy, not so masculine style.

Getting back to Steph and the shop, I began the design of my left arm sleeve. I had pulled an image of a swimsuit model with a fishnet sleeve containing sugar skulls from the internet. The model and her sleeve were beautiful. I wanted that sleeve, with my favorite flowers taking the place of the skulls. Steph said no.

"Why not?" I asked.

"I'm not doing that sleeve on you," she responded.

I didn't quite understand. But she was adamant. I assumed she didn't want to contribute to something that would further feminize my appearance permanently.

I was horribly frustrated. I continued to bring up the fishnet sleeve, but finally moved on to the design of my back: a flogger, similar to that used by the Romans to whip Jesus before he was crucified. The leather straps turned to stems of roses surrounding an amazing portrait of Summer. It was Steph's first portrait. I never hesitated letting her place it on me. While she was doing the work on my back, I brought up the sleeve again. Steph frustratingly said, "I'm not doing a black fishnet on you. It will look horrible. It needs to be blue."

I was stunned. "Is the color of the net what you don't like?!"

"Yes, I'm not doing black."

"I love the idea of blue."

"Then let's do blue."

"My goodness, the disagreement has to do with the color of the stocking. Let's get to work!"

In three sessions, I had my colored fishnet sleeve. I thought to myself that the process was representative of my internal struggle coming to the surface. The right arm was black and white with Scripture and lions to represent the masculine. My left arm was adorned with a fishnet sleeve ornamented with my favorite flowers, representing the feminine. I told myself it was some kind of "individuation"—the Jungian process of becoming a complete person. Fully developing the masculine and feminine aspects of our personalty.

I wasn't acknowledging this internal struggle to anyone. But I knew. Deep down, I knew, and I was digging furiously.

For the last fifteen years, I had been searching for something. I was unsettled. I moved from experience to experience, from accomplishment to accomplishment, from one thing to another with varying degrees of success along the way. But something still eluded me. Triathlon, permaculture design, precious metals, guns, motorcycles—none of them filled the void. My career was amazingly successful, my marriage was solid, secure, and loving. My children were now healthy, the mortgage on the land was paid off and no longer a concern. Yet I still wasn't settled. I needed to start listening. Listening to the thoughts in my own head. I was trapped. In what?!

"Put makeup on me," I blurted out to Summer one evening, as we sat in our bedroom at the ranch. Surprised at the request, she thought this should be fun, and went to work. Foundation, blush, some eye shadow, and lipstick were applied. Not exactly my color palette. She is Native American and I was a good ole white boy. I looked in the mirror and didn't like what I saw in the reflection, a horrible drag queen. I washed up as fast as I could.

Summer told me afterwards, "You would make a pretty lady." Well now, that thought wasn't going to go away anytime soon.

2017 OKLAHOMA SOONERS

BIG 12 CHAMPIONS

12 - 2

THE MAKEOVER

I had decided that during my annual December vacation, with the holidays in full swing, I wanted another full makeover. I did not mean a new skin care routine or an education on preventative aging. I meant a makeover. I wanted to see my face given a radical change in appearance by having a makeup artist create a feminine look with the standard primer, foundation, bronzer, blush, eye shadow, and lipstick. The Harley-riding, cattle-ranching husband and father was digging faster and faster. This obsession was not going away.

With our intimacy and trust having grown so deeply over the last sixteen months, I again expressed to Summer my desire to see how I would appear with a feminine look. "I want to have one of the cosmetic girls give me a makeover at Ulta," I told her. This was a statement of what was going to be happening, not what I wished to have happen. Summer knew that once something grabbed my attention, following it through to conclusion was a given. I had no idea what the outcome of this obsession would be, but I needed to know.

The Ulta store in Norman, Oklahoma was slammed as usual in the final weekend before Christmas. The checkout lines wrapped around the aisles, with women of all ages elfing and selfing. Gift boxes, new formulas for standard makeup products, and restocked items were piled high and being scooped up fast. The cosmetic company representatives were in full force, sampling and answering questions from moms, sisters, sorority girls, and gifting husbands. And I wanted a full makeover that day.

I had already done my "walk through" and knew who I would ask to do this for me. Summer wasn't exactly doing back flips of excitement to go with me, but trying to maintain some sense of control in a situation where her husband was acting so out of his character, she rolled with the changes. I imagined that from her perspective it must have been akin to watching a car wreck develop in slow motion, with no ability to stop it.

The Clinique section is where I put myself, because I had heard of the brand. The rep was pleasing, pregnant, and the kindest young lady I could have encountered that cold day in December. Heart pounding, I waited for her to have a break between customers. Finally getting an opportunity, I moved in quickly to ask, "Could I bother you to help me today?"

"Yeah! What I can I do?"

"I want a makeover. Could you help me with that?" I was going to be crystal clear, and I clarified before she even answered, "I want to look like a girl."

"I can do that. I may need to break away if someone needs something, but sure."

"That would be great." I was pleasantly surprised. My heart rate dropped into the normal zone, and it was then that I first realized that this encounter was the first of many where it would be extremely difficult to surprise the younger generation with personal revelations of any sort.

Our individual differences are so acceptable at this point, that having a defined "normal" can be highly problematic. In a culture where obesity is the norm in physical appearance, crushing debt is normal in our financial affairs, the faithful are extremists, and half the marriages end in divorce, "normal" may not be good and what is good may not be normal. We may actually have more personal freedom than ever before, and not know what to do with it.

I hopped up onto the counter stool, eager to get started. Summer walked around, looking at many of the different products launched for the holiday gifting season. As she kept an eye on me, I watched every shopper blowing through the store that afternoon who was remotely within my line of sight. My eyes darted all over the store looking for a familiar face as the makeup artist started to apply some primer, the first step before laying on the foundation of a new look. This was the town I had lived in for years. I was highly likely to run into someone I knew on one of the last Saturdays before Christmas.

She brushed bronzer from under my temples to my cheekbones, giving me depth and shape. My face was narrow and could use the shadows. She used blush for the sweet pink color on the cheekbone, and finished phase one with the placement of concealer under my eyes to brighten the dark circles that had formed there over the years.

My complexion was smooth and evened out. It was nice, and younger-looking. "I'm doing your eyes now," she said as she brushed some eye primer onto my eyelids to hold the different shades of shadow that would follow. The impact would be here. Many of the striking faces we love in photos and picture in our minds are imprinted into our memories because of a woman's piercing eyes.

"Teach me as you go," I requested.

"Of course," she replied. "The primer will hold the shadows from the palette as I apply them." She applied bronzer as a light shadow across the lids first. "This will be the base layer and give a nice color to the overall lid. I'm following with a slightly darker shadow into the crease of your eyes." My eyelids were hooded more than average for a guy. "We need to create some depth with the next two colors." She was blending the colors with some shimmer as I saw someone I recognized.

Oh my gosh, I know that girl from somewhere, I thought as I spotted a woman I was acquainted with one aisle over trying to get the next thing on her shopping list. She never even looked my way. The teaching continued. Summer had meandered back to us and was now listening.

The sales rep hit my lashes with some mascara to finish my eyes and moved to the lips. This is where the feeling of going "all in" hit me. It's not unusual to see men wearing makeup or eyeshadow. Rock stars need the alluring look for their crazy fans and media personalities need the even foundations for the television cameras. Under her guidance, I applied a nice neutral color to accentuate a pleasing, soft look that I would be leaving with that afternoon.

In hindsight, this was a normal routine that most professional women would go through before taking on the day ahead. It was slightly less than I do now for a date night or an evening function. As she finished, I said,

"I need you to write down exactly what you did so that I can practice this look." Seemed to me like a tall order. It was not.

"For sure!" she said. She pulled a map of a generic face out of her drawer of supplies and started writing down notes with arrows and bullet points. Meanwhile, I looked at my face from all angles in every mirror in my vicinity. I was fascinated, and I liked what I saw looking back. A lot. Samples of everything she used for my makeover were tossed into a bag for both Summer and I to experiment with, and we headed to the checkout line that wound through the aisles. Every few feet there was another mirror for me check myself out in. Another replacement hair dryer for Summer was added to our purchase, and we headed for the door, me wearing my Harley-Davidson beanie and a nice complexion on my face. I had just dug a little deeper.

The trip back to the ranch took thirty minutes. Pulling into the drive, one of us got out to swing the pipe gate off the drive, get the mail, and walk up to the house. As usual, the dogs greeted us at the door by circling us, asking for attention, and getting it before we could settle in at home. I headed straight back to the master bedroom.

Previous to the Ulta trip, before an evening with my parents, I had bought a couple of wigs at a small shop in the north central part of Oklahoma City. The staff there were so kind and patient while Summer and I asked questions about the types, pricing, and care of synthetic hair. It was an early evening outing of laughing, saying "yes" and "no" while each of us tried different styles and colors. Summer lost her fear of turning gray after seeing herself in a strikingly elegant look, while I simply enjoyed seeing hair on my head again. The evening ended with me deciding to leave with a blonde, touching-the-shoulder wig, a color which I wear to this day, and a rich brown just-past-the-shoulder length. The brown brought back memories of my natural color when I was a kid.

My hair was so thick when was in my teens, I looked as if I was wearing a little brown helmet. I would carry a comb in my back pocket to keep that eighties feathered hair neatly parted a bit left of center. It wasn't long after graduation from high school that I started losing my hair to male pattern baldness. The difference from the beginning of my freshman year in college to my graduation was stark. It never bothered me much, though, and I wasn't the only fraternity brother that dealt with a rapidly receding hairline. Thankfully, it wasn't so fast that I missed the long hair phase. I would ride my Nighthawk 650, my long locks waving out from under my helmet. The eighties rocker look didn't last long, but I suppose, looking back, it wasn't the last of the long hair. I just had to wait thirty years to style it that way again.

Back in the house, I swept through the living room with my freshly made-up face, saying "Hey, Maso!" as I blew past my daughter, never looking in her direction. "Hey, Dad," she answered. I entered the bedroom and shut the door. This was going to be a first. I had just had the makeover that I wanted, and now I was actually going to see what I looked like with my blonde hair combined with an even, matched foundation, eye shadow, and lipstick. I pulled the hair from the box labeled "Malibu Blonde" and combed through it a couple of times. I held it upside down and leaned over into it, putting my forehead in first, and pulled it on. When I could feel that it was straight and secure, I stood up and flipped my hair back. I walked over to the mirror to check myself out.

I had spent my life in front of the mirror, brushing my teeth, combing my hair, and shaving every day. I cared deeply about my appearance. In high school, I worked to buy Levi 501s paired with Cole Haan penny loafers. I bought polo shirts and shorts in the preppy phase of the 1980s. I graduated from the University of Oklahoma into Big Pharma wearing beautiful navy, olive, and charcoal suits every day in the field. At that time, I was still working through the week in newer suits, anxious to get home and change into my jeans, boots, and leather jackets for day trips on my Harley or BMW motorcycles. Whatever chase I was involved in, the outfit had to look damn good.

As I looked at my reflection, I was stunned. I was looking into the face of someone looking back as if they had spent years alone with buried treasure, waiting to be discovered and then, suddenly, found. The moment was like a scene from a movie. The previous sixteen months, the confiding of previously unknown thoughts with Summer, seemingly senseless purchases, and a metrosexual fashion style all now made sense. That had all been the relentless banging of a deeply personal inner struggle inside of me, knowing discovery was close. I now stared at that face, discovered, and saw myself. As the foundation was going on, my costume was coming off. I had dug deep and relentlessly. I had found myself and my treasure. The personal tension that moved me from triathlon to permaculture design, from the city to the country, from riding motorcycles to grazing cattle, had culminated with who I found in the mirror. Staring back was an attractive, blonde, blue-eyed woman.

That treasure would take me on a journey that would change my life. The image staring back would lead me the rest of the way on a quest of living unapologetically and authentically in my personal dealings, saying "yes" to professional opportunities, and living in alignment with what I deeply wanted for myself and presenting that to the world. As I stared into the shadowed eyes, I had no idea then how all that would happen. But that treasure would not be put back.

2018 OKLAHOMA SOONERS
BIG 12 CHAMPIONS
12 - 2

COMFORT IN DISCOMFORT

I had found the next all-consuming thing to immerse myself in. It was that pesky treasure find in the mirror. I was now acting out, by making women's apparel purchases that seemingly made no sense at all. As my closet underwent a radical transformation within a few months, Summer became more stressed and kept incredulously asking, "When and where are you going to wear that stuff?" I would irritatedly answer, "I'll get it worn!"

Consciously, I had no idea when. But subconsciously and methodically, I kept piecing together a wardrobe that would be the envy of any woman outside of New York or Beverly Hills.

I had an excellent grasp of the fashion style I was comfortable with wearing. I regularly made purchases for what, looking in the rearview mirror, were so clearly test runs. By the spring, I gave little thought to what those around me might or might not be thinking, as I made wardrobe purchases for a completely different life that I wasn't ready to step into or allowing myself to acknowledge.

She knew. Deep down, she knew. Ever since the weekend we had spent together confiding our future hopes and dreams to each other, Summer had known where this was headed. She had seen me nurturing the feminine side for months. I was willingly letting her take on leadership roles in our relationship that I had tightly held onto for years—the finances, daily decisions, the vacation and holiday planning. These were the familiar male roles I had held and I was happy letting them go. I was secure in our relationship and Summer was so capable of caring for us as a family, that I was making an internal gender transition before I was ready to admit that's what this was.

I had lived an amazing life for over fifty years as a happy little boy playing with GI Joes, and collecting football cards and *Avengers* comic books. I mowed lawns through high school, drank beer, and was a disruptive teen with the rest of the guys. I attended the University of Oklahoma so I could see the Sooners play every football game, joined a fraternity, was at the gym bodybuilding daily, and got married after I graduated college. Joining the pharmaceutical industry, having quick success there, and purchasing a home, the American Dream had played out in real time for me. Sexuality? My heterosexuality was never questioned. Not by me or anyone else that I knew.

This level of personal achievement went on for years. I finally realized, at some point later, that I wasn't going to find more answers by adding to this list of achievements, or at least not until I figured out what my purpose was for the rest of my life.

The discovery of the woman in the mirror was a huge turning point for me. I would later be able to articulate it better. The purpose and meaning of life is found in the experience of it. In saying "yes" to all my different experiences, I was able to get to a point in my own hero's journey where I could leave the Harley-riding, cattle-ranching man behind and embark on some grand adventure that reads like a novel.

What the hell triggered all of this? The younger person of today who seeks to live differently seems to know something isn't "right" early. But with me, something triggered an affirmation—an event that feels right and/or good. It was that damn second makeover and the resulting look in the mirror. The discovery of that, wondering if it was obtainable, combined with the entrenchment of a wonderful life as a man, left me in turmoil for months.

Until then, I rode those motorcycles and worked the cattle daily. At the same time, I was experiencing a new sense of what letting go might look like in the future. It was mental. It was different. It was a tug of war. For instance, I was still as relentless as ever in my pursuit of my fitness. But my workouts moved from bench presses, bicep curls, and tricep extensions to barbell squats, donkey kicks, and core work. I began to lay off the shoulder exercises and start a feminine shaping process that I wouldn't admit to for months.

I finally made my first outing dressed as a woman to the drive-in for a Coke. Dressed in skinny jeans, a red top, and heels, I made the drive through town, ordered my Coke and survived. A couple of weeks later, I planned and made a trip to the mall. Walking through the mall, I almost tripped in my wedges on the steps visiting a familiar boutique, and my heart rate skyrocketed. *Who the hell just saw that?!* I asked myself. Looking around, I wasn't aware of anyone. Thank God. In the boutique, I was unrecognizable to the staff that had seen me in my normal guy mode making the wardrobe purchases. Blonde hair, new makeup routine in play, and the chic fashion had done the job. They were shocked when I revealed the truth, and loved on me, encouraging me. I'd survived round two. I left the mall with a couple of double-takes while stopped at the light. Obviously, my look left a favorable impression.

Summer went along with me dressed in my new style for a couple of lunch dates over the course of the next few months. I thought that choosing restaurants with a more "liberal" and younger crowd might be the easiest establishments if I was planning on staying publicly in one place for any considerable length of time. But I was wrong. The first was more of a singles spot where every person of the opposite sex is thoroughly reviewed upon entering. Wearing a jean skirt, peach sleeveless blouse, and wedges, I walked in the front entrance, with Summer following me. I felt the gazes and never slowed down. We went straight out the back door. That wasn't going to be for me. Not yet. We settled on an outdoor bar in the Paseo Arts District of Oklahoma City. It was a great experience; people were simply indifferent to me and behaving normally. Whatever hesitancy I'd had about being in public disappeared.

Summer recalled thinking this was the the time I was becoming who I might've been had I not followed the script over the last half of my life. It was an interesting observation and significant, as she started processing what was taking place with the two of us.

One more uneventful day trip for burgers and I decided that I didn't have to keep wondering about a public transition. The turmoil wasn't going to wane anytime soon; I just wasn't going to worry about what people in public were thinking. Because I realized they weren't thinking about me.

Summer shared many of the feelings she experienced as I was transitioning. The insecurities from her youth and being surrounded by little, blue-eyed girls with bigger boobs. I shared the feelings of intellectual honesty with her. "I don't feel like a woman trapped in a man's body. I feel like a man in a man's body, wanting to be a woman."

Summer responded, "You're a man in a man's body, exhausted. The woman inside is saying 'Move over, I'm driving this bus!'"

***

My career was still at a high point and I had won the top award again. Two years in row. The repeat was uncommon, because the next year's goal is based on the previous year's winning results. As a reward, we had a corporate trip to Cabo. That would be interesting.

My style had definitely shifted and was clearly obvious to my colleagues. I simply didn't care what they thought about me and my outward change. I had made the internal shift needed if I was to move forward. To my pleasant surprise, the trip turned out great. We stayed at the pool daily from mid-morning until the time came to prep ourselves for dinner. Pineapple mojitos and iguanas surrounded us. The mojitos were amazing and the lizards were like pets. Alternating between the sun and shade, I wore my swim trunks and a woman's T-shirt. Summer and I enjoyed a day at the spa and ended the trip with a pedicure. And pink toes.

The disconnection and struggle was finding myself sprinting from one weekend to the next, simply to find the feelings of "alignment" again. It wasn't about wanting to be "girlie." It was about wanting what I was on the outside to match the inside. I had placed myself in situations for the last few months that seemed like tests of my resolve. Situations that would be normal for anyone, like dining out. Important dinners, banquets, and reward presentations in my profession. Nothing deterred me. My mind was on the future: I could do this. But not as a guy dressed as a woman. Dabbling wasn't enough. Frustration was setting in and I thought it was easier to be in guy mode than be in in the middle, with no resolution. If I did this, though, it would be a massive life transition.

TEAM PRIDE?

The trip with Summer temporarily broke up the march towards transition. When I recollect back to that time frame, I can easily see what would've appeared to be so much confusion and questioning, for lack of a better phrase, in regards to my appearance. It must've been rough for Summer to be living with the changes that outside observers were witnessing and most assuredly discussing with whispers. As I marched on, determined to see where this path would lead, she never left my side. As we returned from Cabo, events were advancing rapidly towards a conclusion that Summer could see coming long before I would admit them. I continued to plan, purchase, and prepare for a new identity no matter how much I denied or hid it.

Summer had several conversations with her sister during this time. Her sister had stayed at the ranch while we were in Cabo. She brought her up to speed on the status of our life at home. She filled her in on what was in the closet regarding my wardrobe, my hair, and showed her pictures. She ended the conversation with humor. "You know the positives if this keeps building. Boobs are coming, and everyone loves boobs."

Continuing to dig, uncover, and expose the hidden treasure led to an opportunity for me to step into the public setting with little thought to what that would mean by attending the annual Pride parade. I could wander in the crowd without being too self-conscious. I could dip my toe into the pool of group identity, and what the celebration of that might look like in the future.

Summer reluctantly agreed to go with me to the event. We met up with another couple that I had met out shopping while piecing my new wardrobe together. They were two women who had been together for several years and had to suffer the loss of family connections and their roles within the church due to their commitment to each other. Arriving in the area and wading through the crowd, I had little concern to being seen in the yellow column dress from Banana Republic, accessorized with the white Polo belt and Coach shoes. This was the beginning of what I refer to as my "awkward phase." The point where I moved from discovery and planning to doing. If I was going bring the woman staring back at me from the mirror to the world, I had some fucking work ahead of me to make that happen. At this point, I was just a guy putting his first foot forward on this journey. I knew it had to be done. But I wouldn't linger on the path.

We visited vendor booths, looking at brochures for LGBT-friendly businesses, and I noted that I had not dealt with many of the struggles that others in the LGBT community encountered daily. I felt I had little in common with most of the festival attendees. Our group soon found ourselves in the shade of a canopy along the parade route, and waited for the procession.

As the parade came through, we watched the cars, trucks, and floats loaded with celebrants, waving, tossing candy, and enjoying their inclusion in the event. It was people-watching at its finest. Leather-clad men in chains, drag queens singing, and corporate sponsors showing their support of all things rainbow made up the bulk of the participants. Summer was sitting in the shade of the canopy, giving this experience a fair shot. But we were both out of our element. Summer and I weren't part of the community. She was struggling tremendously with what the potential change I was making would mean to her and her identity. She wasn't attracted to women and the thought of taking on the *L* due to my choices unsettled her, to say the least.

I wasn't really fired up about being part of any group. I certainly wasn't ready to adopt the celebration of group identity. This wasn't new. In my previous endeavors, I'd grazed my cattle differently than other ranchers, my triathlon training was different because I always trained alone, and I had my own personal relationship with God. One that differed from what I heard from the "church," and the two didn't quite mesh.

The parade ended, we grabbed a bite to eat with the girls, and caught an Uber back to the hotel. There we laid on the bed, relaxed, and talked about the day. We weren't happy with the experience, but we had some answers to questions about the path ahead of us. We napped and then changed for a dinner out. We talked over pizza about where this might lead. Wherever that was, it still wouldn't be as part of a group, no matter how much or little we might have in common. I just wasn't geared that way. I did things alone.

Before the day began, I had wanted to experience the event with a "view from the field of play," wondering if I had a "team." I left the day recognizing that while I might not know exactly how I would choose to live in the future, I did know that I was unique and had found more joy over the last fifteen years marching in my own parade of life experiences to the beat of my own drum. I would continue down the road less traveled. Summer and I would find our way forward. I knew what I needed. Team Andrea needed to be built. But it wouldn't be carrying a flag. Of any color.

OUT OF THE BOX

The heat of the Oklahoma summer at the ranch was becoming unbearable. Half the orchard was dead. We couldn't water, mulch, or care for the trees enough to choose pushing forward with a producing enterprise. Summer's shoulder had finally recovered from surgery and with my continuing success in the pharma industry, we weren't willing to take another run at Mother Nature with the orchard. We didn't see it as a failure. It was just an appreciation of the work it takes to bring produce to our kitchens.

I realized that the freight train of possible transition was barreling down on me and I was at the crossroads of choosing to live as a woman the rest of my life or making the decision to say no, and chalk up another life-learning experience. The working trip to Cabo had me comfortable enough with the relationships I had with my colleagues. A transition would be fine. The company was progressive regarding diversity in the workplace. So no worries about my employment being in danger. My clients had seen my style change, and I believed if I moved forward with a gender swap, some of their questions would be answered.

If I didn't move forward, I was going to leave the woman from the mirror buried with whatever treasure she had with her. This was gut-wrenching. I knew that I didn't want to live with the knowledge of what was available to me and saying "no." I didn't want to get any older and say "I wish I would've ..."

Yet I already had a woman who I considered a treasure. Summer was in the middle of a long hot season of seeing the death of a seventeen-year marriage. Our story had previously appeared to be on a trajectory of growing old together and following the well-known script that plays out with a well-known ending.

Daily, I drove the final fifty miles after my last client visit deep in thought. I would come up the gravel drive in the late afternoon to pull into the garage. The dogs would bark and circle the vehicles, and I would drive slowly so as to not run them over. They would excitedly wait for my exit from the truck to greet me, every time. Summer would hear the barking, put the door up, and help me unload the vehicle of now-empty containers that had been full of snacks and meals at the start of the day. Almost every day. This particular afternoon, I knew that I had reached a point of no return. I had to communicate how I had broken down my current gender situation. Day after day, the drama of my inner struggle would play out in my head or in the bedroom. It was always center stage. Being a self-proclaimed lover of analogies to make my points, I came up with one that would help me communicate this particular situation and where I found myself.

Before we unloaded the car, I asked my wife to not go back in the house right away. "I need you to know where I think we currently find ourselves," I told her. "Please listen to how I feel about this. I'm exhausted and broken!"

"I'm tired, too. This is going on and on. It can't keep going like this!" she responded loudly. "I'm going to lose my husband. He's becoming a woman. I'm straight! Not a lesbian! I like Andy! I'm sorry you don't."

"This pose I'm holding day after day is exhausting me!" I said loudly back. "I know that what I have been searching for is right in front of me. I don't know what the road forward looks like for me, but I can't go back to where I have been. I won't go back knowing what I know! I can do this! I have to and I want you with me." Standing in front of my lifted Toyota Tacoma, I was now sobbing and yelling. "I can't move forward with indecision anymore. You have to move forward too! Let's just do it together. The tires are all flat on this thing. I'm not taking this vehicle (me) any further. Yelling at each other won't help fix me any faster! Your worst fears won't be realized! The worst is behind us. I'm trying to fix this. Help me!"

We were both exasperated. I was wiping my tears as she composed herself to walk back inside. Turning back to me, she said, "I'm not leaving you or going anywhere." Picking my belongings off the chest freezer, she was finished. We went inside. I had cattle to move in the pasture.

***

In my journaling, I sketched a representation of where I found myself at this time. I had been in a box. We all are in boxes. We keep ourselves in these familiar, secure, little boxes that we create for ourselves throughout the course of our lives. Sometimes, others help us build them. Our families, our friends, our careers, are influential in keeping us where everyone is content. In little boxes. Living in the box I had made allowed me to attain success in my career, a debt-free life, a wonderful family, and fit the mold of the All-American life. The second image illustrated the last two years. Living as if I had cut a hole in the side of the box, venturing out, never getting too far from my comfy box. I couldn't; I had a chain around my ankle. Realizing that I could temporarily remove the chain wasn't good enough. The last image was a box that had been cut down at all four corners. It was lying open, all four sides flattened out. It was unusable. It couldn't contain me anymore. Pictured next to the box was a little red wagon loaded with what I wanted to take with me. Pulling the wagon, I wasn't going back into a box.

The heat was waning, and OU football would kick off another season of high hopes for another run at the national championship. Football season, Halloween, my birthday, Thanksgiving, and Christmas would give us all the usual reasons to celebrate with each other and our families. But the next four months would be massively different than the years that came before.

I had decided to say "yes," and I had some work to do.

DO YOU STILL LIKE FOOTBALL?

On a beautiful September day in Oklahoma, I hosted a lunch for a clinic full of doctors and their staffs. I was nervous the entire lunch. Not for the appointment; the subject matter was routine. I was nervous because I was going to see my parents as soon as lunch ended, and have a conversation that would change their lives.

I had prepared cards filled with notes that contained my talking points; I wanted to make sure not to miss saying anything. I was thoughtful and deliberate with how I wanted to deliver the news. As I presented information to the providers at my lunch about the anticoagulant that I represented, I fidgeted with my note cards, reviewing them at every opportunity. When the last of my guests left the conference room, my nervousness hit a new high.

I reached down into the bag, grabbed my phone, and called my mom. She answered and I asked if they were at home. "Yeah, yeah, we're at home," she told me.

"I'm going to come by for a few minutes to visit," I told her. "We'll be here," was the response. Were someone monitoring me, my vital signs would definitely be showing signs of stress. This conversation was actually going to happen. My heart was pounding. I packed my presentation materials, politely exited the offices, and hustled to my vehicle.

Their home was about fifteen minutes from the clinic. I loved going home. Every time. It was always comforting to take the final corner into the neighborhood and turn into the drive. The home I grew up in was shaded by massive trees covering the yard that I mowed as a kid. Now, fifty years later, I shut off the car, took a deep breath, and grabbed the iPad.

I walked a little faster up the stone path to the front door, took the final two steps, and was met by my mother holding the door open. Nervous, I hugged Mom. She said, "Your dad just left to run an errand." My knees about buckled. *Good grief*, I thought. I had just called to see if they were around and told them that I would be coming by the house. Errand-running for my dad could last anywhere from fifteen minutes to a few hours.

The inside of their home bore little resemblance to the house where I was raised. Continuous updating had kept it feeling modern and on-trend for them as they aged gracefully. It still felt like home, though, as it did the day before I left for college. I walked with Mom towards the dining room and the large table where many important discussions had taken place. Announcements of impending divorce, cancer diagnosis, and holiday celebrations were held in chairs around that table.

Today, another conversation would occur. It was game time. The clock had started, the ball was now in motion, and Summer and I were leaving for San Antonio in a few days, where we would take a path completely unforeseen to us a couple of years previous.

"Come here and sit down, I want to talk to you about something." This was unusual, and with my family being very supportive and open about health issues, I didn't want to scare her, so I immediately continued, "I'm not sick; all is well. Summer and I are good. I want to talk about me. I'm going to tell you some things and show you some pictures. I want you to look and listen." I pulled out my tablet and propped it open on the table. I had all the pictures from the last several months on it. Hair, makeup, clothes, all the changes that I'd made to myself temporarily for the last six months, would all be in front of my mother on the iPad screen. I pulled out my note cards. "Hold your questions," I said, not slowing down. "I know you guys have seen my 'style' change. The pictures are more authentic than you know. This isn't a fetish, crossdressing, or sexual. This is the way you'll see me in the future. I'm going to transition to living as a woman." She just stared at me. It was all out now! I must have been talking at lightning speed. I continued, answering questions she hadn't asked, "I'm exhausted going back and forth. Not everybody that transitions feels like they've known their whole life."

Mom sat in silence. Her eyes were glistening, and just then front door opened, and my dad walked in.

"Hey, Andy! What's going on?"

Mom didn't miss a beat. "Bill, you better get in here."

I got up, and went towards the door to herd him to the dining table. "I came to see you guys and talk to you about something." I asked my dad to sit down and began again. It was good for my mom, sitting there in shock, to hear it again. Assuring him that I wasn't sick, I repeated the main points and continued with them both, "This is how I have been at home for most of this last year. This is me most of the time out of the public eye. But I've been going out more recently. It's getting more as time goes on and it's going to be all the time."

I was done with this being a private matter. It wasn't unreasonable to think that I would eventually run into my parents' friends, or have them see me and Summer out for lunch, dinner, or shopping. My parents have quite a social network and a large group of close friends.

Mom looked intently at the images. Reflecting back, I wasn't pretty. I looked like a guy with hair and makeup. But I was happy enough then to show my parents the pictures. I didn't realize, early in my transition, how powerful we can be in manifesting the vision we want for ourselves. I would eventually pull myself from the mirror. These pictures were just the beginning.

Dad had been a Navy man, flying in the Korean War, and a former baseball and football player; we connected easily on all the masculine things we enjoyed together. My biological father had left me and my mother in Oklahoma when I was a year old. She soon met and married the man that became my dad, whose family was of German heritage. The work ethic they brought from eastern Europe carried them out of the Depression and through World War II. Dad's time as an airman in Korea, followed by a long career in the Department of Defense and a series of stints with different contractors, instilled a sense of discipline that he modeled for me and my sister. His sense of compassion for those less fortunate than us exhibited Christ more than anything I was taught in a number of churches I would attend over the years.

I had seen examples of goodness my entire life in these two. Many friends, belief systems, life experiences, and political views graced the doors of our home. My parents exposed me to a lot. They loved us deeply and they'd set me off with the wind at my back.

Now, Dad really looked at the images as I hit all my prepared bullet points.

I went through the story of all of us having masculine and feminine aspects of ourselves. Mom, a counselor, was a huge fan of Carl Jung and his methodology for helping patients become a whole person. Jung would've been proud. I told them that I had been driven and searching my whole life for something. What, I had not known. "All the hobbies, guns, motorcycles, prepping for the apocalypse, have consumed me. I've been eaten up with triathlon and ranching; my healthcare career is successful and at a high point. My marriage is great, and the ranch is paid off. I just want to live!" I addressed all the practical things that my parents might think I should take into consideration. The analogies flowed. They would pour out, so as to help them relate to my decision. I was trying to explain to the two of them something that couldn't be understood. "I know neither of you understand. This isn't normal. You're not supposed to understand." This was where me facing reality and taking sole responsibility for my decision would benefit my future. It would help me help others. "I have found myself in what has felt like a costume. The masculine side of me has driven this vehicle and I'm exhausted. The feminine side is going to drive the rest of the way."

I'm not sure how much if not all of that was psychobabble, but with Mom being an expert on Jung's Shadow, I hoped she had a starting point for what I was telling her that afternoon. Though I can't say that Jung was much of a comfort. What I did know was the guy sitting with his parents, pouring out his news, was likely there in their living room for the last time. I have an always been a "tear the band-aid off fast" personality.

All my attention was on my dad, who was still listening closely, silently processing what I was saying and the images I was showing them. He continued to look at my iPad, adjusting his line of sight due to macular degeneration. He stared at the photos, looked up at me, and again at the screen. He slowly lifted his head and looked me in the eyes.

With tears forming, he slowly and intently asked me, "Do you still like football?"

This was the exact point in the discussion when I knew everything would be okay. "Yes! I still like football."

My dad would have had his world rocked more had I said "no" to that question than to my revelation that I was going to live as a woman. We had lived football in our home for as long as I can remember. A "no" answer would have upset his worldview and all he knew to be true. The love of football and what we share was an undeniable truth that spoke to who we really are and had been our whole lives. All he would've known, believed, or experienced with me would've been a lie. While he had just received life-changing news about his family, he knew, at the heart of the situation, that my gender presentation didn't really matter.

The three of us relaxed. We could now talk. I went through all I knew about transition. We talked about every transition being unique and different. Each person with different reasons and of different ages. The thoughts and feelings experienced, the acceptance, denial, and the level of support each person feels is different.

In the end, no one else's transition mattered.

I asked them to let me reveal this to the rest of our family on my timeline. Discussions of this type could be exhausting. Our extended family was out of state and I didn't have a sense of urgency to continue with informing them at this point. I would inform my sister within a day. "Talk to your friends," I told them. They would need their close knit-network over the next few months as they processed what they learned that afternoon. I had to get back to work.

As I gathered my things to leave, it was always normal for Mom to collect various items for me to take home. She would send me home with leftovers, things for Summer, magazines they had already read, and many other things that that she didn't want to throw away. They walked me out, as usual, onto the porch and to the car. Mom was carrying a grocery sack of items that had been set aside for me. As I started the engine to leave, she held up the sack. "I guess I don't need to keep saving these for you anymore."

"Why? What are they?"

"*Men's Journals.*"

She laughed. We laughed. Our sense of humor was intact. All was well. Would be well. They would continue to love me unconditionally. It was just going to take awhile for them to process the changes that were coming to their lives.

My lunch hour ended with that lunch. Is it any wonder I was exhausted?

Years later, they haven't changed. As they go through the aging process together in a healthy and honest way, my gender identity never changed the love they have for me and the love I feel from them.

Oh, and we still talk football.

THE ALAMO

After telling my parents about my transition, things began to move at lightning speed. I reviewed the situation with my therapist, Miranda. She informed me that she had never seen someone move so fast and decisively. Normally, she would be concerned with the speed of the developments. But in this situation she had never seen someone so poised and ready to make the transition. That wasn't a surprise to me. I had a history of assessing and analyzing situations thoroughly, moving swiftly to put decisions and plans into motion. Now, Summer and I were headed to San Antonio. This would be his last stand.

***

My wife Summer is an amazing woman. She danced her way through childhood, adolescence, and right into the dance program at the University of Oklahoma. The talent for dance and hard work that she had developed from an early age was fostered by loving grandparents and a mentor in the university's department of dance. Working and saving to pay her tuition and fees, she would sit out semesters until she had saved enough again to pick up where she left off. Working at the dance academy during one of these times, she and I started our dance before I knew the music was playing.

To hear her tell the story, anyone listening would hear her infatuation with the nice man who dropped his daughter off at the studio, sometimes watch at the observation window, and always be on time to pick her up after class. His daughter would dance all year long, get to the final performance at the spring recital, and not go onstage in the final piece. She was younger than the others and he was there to take her and have her try again the next year. He was so patient and good with the little girl. She told her friends she would marry him. She just had to wait until he figured that out. Several years of their dance followed. It included a brief narcissistic relationship that left him and his daughter scarred. He was now back in a routine of dropping off and picking up with plenty of opportunity to make small talk. At last, he took one.

Now, my transition from her husband to her wife was coming to pass. Summer had to do something for herself. The changes we were going through were consuming our lives. And they were sucking all of the oxygen out of our relationship. Summer loved to be in the kitchen making art: baking, cooking, and experimenting with new recipes for the family. This was her stress relief. Her individual cup needed a refill, and taking a baking class out of town might offer some personal growth for her. The Culinary Institute of America has several locations around the country and offers different classes throughout the year. There was a week-long baking class being offered in San Antonio that fall. She enrolled for the four-day course, we made travel arrangements, got care for the ranch and our daughter, and headed south several weeks later.

From our place in Noble, Oklahoma, it was a day trip down to San Antonio. One stoplight on Main Street in Noble was all that might slow you down in getting through town unless you didn't slow to 35 mph, then the small-town police were willing to help out with that problem. We loaded the 4Runner and headed to Texas. To the Alamo.

My purpose was to spend the whole week living as my future self to see if this was something I could step into completely and fast. She would spend her days in class, and I would spend my days in contemplation of what was to come. Hours into the drive south, she asked, "What are you changing your name to?"

"I was thinking Andrea. It's easy on everybody, especially my parents. What do you think?"

"I think it's great. What about your middle name?" she asked. "I have no idea. I want it to flow easy with Andrea."

"The girls have names that begin with *L*," she said. "Let's start there." One of the girls' first names was Lydia, but she used her middle name. The oldest had Lauren as a middle name, and she used her first name. We blew through several options.

"What about Leigh?" I offered, then spelled it. "L E I G H."

"I like it. A lot."

"Andrea Leigh, Andrea Leigh, Andrea Leigh," then: "Andi Leigh." She loved how it rolled for her, and that was the process. Quick and easy. I had my new name. A name that would be easy for my family and friends, a middle name that flowed easily from the first. It could also be used as a last name going forward, for social and business purposes.

She asked me another question on this leg of the trip. "Have you thought about what kind of woman you want to be?"

Good question. I knew. I just didn't want to say.

I couldn't quite nail down how I would make the change professionally. As we drove towards Texas, I said to Summer, "I have had a great career with a lot of wins. I want to win as a woman." My career was the one area in which, despite my being on the verge of finalizing how I was going to spend the rest of my life personally, I couldn't quite nail down how I would make the change.

"Just be yourself. All your clients love you," she responded.

Sounded humorous to hear "just be yourself" before I had switched genders. But she was right.

I was welcome and had privileges in many clinics where restrictions on pharmaceutical representatives had gone into place years before. I had travelled Oklahoma as the point person for some of the biggest medications in the pharmaceutical business over the last twenty years. "I think I will just tell them right up front. They won't have to wonder anymore what's going on with me. They will have seen my style change over the last couple of years, and I will bring them along for the ride. I see most of them every couple of weeks. If I miss them when I have an appointment or can't get to one for a few weeks, I'll have one or two more opportunities. I don't want to miss them completely. I want a chance to see them again. I'll start the process early."

Summer's idea was a great one. We decided to bring my clients on the final leg of the journey, and I'd begin the process shortly after returning from our trip south.

We arrived in downtown San Antonio as planned. Staying in an older hotel across the street from the famous Alamo, we parked on the street for a quick check-in and had the vehicle valet parked. Multiple suitcases and twenty-one pairs of shoes were unloaded onto the luggage cart. Twenty-one. All mine. I joked that the HRT was already having the first profound effect on me with my indecision on what shoes to take. So I just took them all. Well, most. Checked in, room keys gathered, we headed to the elevators and our rooms. We would make this our home base for the next several days and relax after our travel from Oklahoma.

As we got ready to head to dinner, I realized that I had left my sunglasses in the vehicle. If you have followed me on social media, you'll know that I rarely am without my sunglasses on my head. My version of a headband, they are what I refer to as a "big girl bow." I love the look. This started early in my transition. "I'm going to get my sunglasses out of the car. I'll meet you downstairs."

I went to the valet stand and asked for my keys. "I left my white sunglasses in the car and need them for our walk."

"The car is a couple of blocks away; we'll go get them for you," they responded.

"If you don't mind, that would be lovely." And off they went.

As I waited for them to return, Summer joined me. "Did you get your sunglasses?"

"I did. The boys were happy to go get them."

Looking incredulous, she asked, "Are you kidding me?! You would've never paid a valet to go get my sunglasses had I left mine in the car. You would've gone and got them yourself. You're such a princess!"

"Well, I paid them to go get them." Pausing, I then answered the earlier question. "I guess that's the kind of woman I want to be." I had decided that I would ask for what I wanted moving forward.

For the next week, Summer would Uber over to the Culinary Institute for her days in the kitchen and I would get ready for mine as Andrea. I would go for a walk in the mornings, and make my way across the street to the grounds of the Alamo. I would sit in the park surrounding the museum and relax. I contemplated the changes headed my way. With no second thoughts, I realized this was the path for me. Despite losing a shoe as I crossed an intersection, I was at peace. I sat for hours each day with the realization that I would get to be a different person for the rest of my life. What an opportunity. I would do this right.

We would meet in the late afternoon, talk about her day in the kitchens of the Institute, and walk to dinner or head off to one of the establishments we had wanted to try around San Antonio. Summer recalled later that it was on one of these walks to dinner around the city that for the first time she experienced the feelings of not being with a guy to protect her, and later thinking about the tension of how much she had wanted to hold my hand and how much she didn't. "I had always been with a man, and from then on it was two women."

When we met back at the end of day one, I had flowers waiting for her, and she cried tears of joy recalling the day. Finally, she was having an experience of her own.

The second night of this "vacation," she asked if we could go out as a regular married couple, husband and wife. We meandered down to the River Walk to have a barbecue dinner after her day at school and my day of being alone in my thoughts. I was wearing a blue polo shirt and an orange hat. Summer was alone in the knowledge that this was likely one of her last meals with her husband on vacation.

She had a great experience at the Culinary Institute, rekindling a love of baking and fostering her creativity. We packed up all the shoes and the rest of our clothes and headed back north. I had solidified my decision to transition and would begin the formal process upon our return home to Oklahoma. Informing the rest of my family, colleagues, and friends would take time. And a lot of energy.

I already had plans for the physical transition. I knew it would take someone amazingly gifted to bring the picture in my head to life.

ACCEPTANCE AND INDIFFERENCE

I had a mission. I had a preferred time frame for the transition. The timing I desired was from Thanksgiving to Christmas. I would get time away from work for short term leave, and combine it with my annual vacation surrounding the end of year holiday. I had a legal name change to process, consults to schedule with the doctors, and a short term leave to schedule.

This process would be tremendously disruptive and potentially fatal to my family and career relationships. If I was wrong it would be a catastrophic, lifetime-altering move. I would be betting everything. But, I wasn't wrong. I believed in myself. I was intellectually honest and knew what I was doing. I was going all in to win at this game.

My mission began on a Sunday. Plopping down on the sofa, I worked to construct the email in way that would convey my need to meet with my manager at the earliest convenience and also keep my privacy until we spoke in person. I had worked with Jon twice for a total of seven years, with a three-year stint in another therapeutic division between assignments. We had a great relationship, both of us with highly competitive personalities, and a tremendous amount of respect for each other. We could talk about guns and land for hours. Jon was an avid hunter, gun enthusiast, and Alabama football fan. As a manager of a highly efficient team of successful representatives for the premier sales force in the pharmaceutical industry, he genuinely cared and connected with each of us personally. My leadership style of coaching to the individual, in the moment, and transferring my vision of success to my teams later in the fashion industry was heavily influenced by working with him for those years.

With the email written, proofread multiple times, and shared with Summer, I hit send. "Jon, could we set aside some time at the earliest convenience for me to discuss a personal issue?" This was a highly unusual request on a Sunday afternoon. "I'm not sick, Summer and I are good," I wrote. Responding quickly that afternoon, he alleviated any anxiety I might've had about how long it would take to get a meeting scheduled. We would meet the next day at a cafe bakery in South Oklahoma City.

We were both prompt, grabbed some coffee, and went to a booth in the corner that was walled in on three sides. "I really appreciate you meeting with me on short notice," I said as we shook hands. Pharma jobs have a reputation for "flexibility" in how the representatives conduct business. The reputation of starting the day at ten a.m. and ending at two had been well earned by many in the business over the years. But not by those on our team. And most of those days are long gone. The accountability to our teams, partners, and patients really reduced the odds of that being a secure job if you weren't prompt and dependable. We were dependable. And on time. We said our pleasantries and I got down to business.

"Bear with me. You're the first guy friend that I've told this information, and you're my manager. I know you've seen my 'style' change over this last year. Earlier this year I identified as transgender in the HR system. You may have heard this, I don't know. I have been told I'm the most 'out not out' person my friends know. I guess it's an open secret. I don't want it to be a secret anymore and I'm letting you know I want to and plan to transition at work." There it was. I had advanced the ball way down the field on this possession.

Jon continued to listen and take in what I was saying to him as I went on, "My name will be changed in a few weeks and we have some planning to do. I wanted to tell you first, since the guidelines say to 'inform your manager or HR.' I've been on this journey awhile and believe it or not, I'm the most comfortable I've been my entire life. I don't expect you to understand, I just need your support. I've thought about you, the team, our company, and my doctors and nurses. I've got some ideas and timelines in mind. I'm going to take leave along with my vacation and have some 'work' done before the end of the year." The words flowed easily and I could see Jon absorbed it well. I continued, "Help me make what is going to be a challenge as easy as possible. I have done my homework, research, and talked for hours with my team." I meant my personal advisors. "It's real. Who would've thought, years ago?"

I was done. I had said what I intended to say, and set my index cards down.

He replied, "Well, I thought this was what you might want to talk about. I told my wife last night, 'I bet this is what this is all about ...'" He confessed that he didn't know much about the policies from HR. Which was fine. I did, and I was telling him all of this so that we could coordinate coverage on my key accounts, my time away, and how to inform the team. But mostly, because he was my friend. He would give me the support I needed as I took the lead and kept him informed of the process.

With us both being team-first players, we figured out what it would mean for our team. "I think that you should tell each one on the team individually," he suggested. This was not the way the HR policy would read. A statement on a transition date and expected pronoun usage seemed more in line with widely used corporate policies that were now addressing these issues. I thought differently. I would own my stuff.

"I think so, too," I responded.

It was a long conversation. We spoke of the personal aspects of the last two years and the progression of my transition.

Ours was a highly efficient and tenured team. We were skilled at our jobs. Each of us had our individual strengths that allowed us all to excel. My superpower was an ability to relate potentially complicated data and results from landmark studies into clear and concise messages that my clients could take into their own decision making process. And I was direct. I would be direct with each of my teammates.

I started with my closest partner, James. He had watched me change over the last few years and never said a word to me. We communicated multiple times a day about product messaging, client follow up, and our individual itineraries for our shared clients. We co-hosted multiple lunches each month for our providers. The day after informing Jon of my intentions, James and I were departing from a lunch we had just hosted. I asked if I could chat with him a moment about something. I jumped into the front seat of his car, invading his space. He immediately asked, "Are you sick or something?"

Laughing, I said, "No, I'm going to transition to a woman."

He paused awkwardly and responded with an outstretched hand and said, "Okay, congratulations." A few more words that expressed his relief that I wasn't leaving the company or terminally ill, and we were done. He shook my hand, we moved on, and never missed a beat as a partnership. The utmost professional representative, my transition was seamless with him and the success that followed for us for several more years was not a surprise.

I called Trent next. Technically the best representative that I had the pleasure of working with during my career, he met me for coffee later in the afternoon. "You're still the same on the inside, aren't you?" he responded.

"Yes, but the gossip could affect you on the job," I said.

I think he welcomed the challenge of any opportunity that might give him a chance at more time to talk in the offices.

"I'm sure going to look different," I said, and ended it.

The rest of the team sang the same song and I appreciated it. "You have my support," "I am so pleased you called to tell me," "Thanks for sharing that with me." These are the responses that I heard from one colleague after another. A cohesive, efficient, successful team of eleven. Eight conservative white guys in Oklahoma responding to what I told them and accepting me. My female counterparts welcomed me to the club.

This was precedent-setting for the company. Or it should've been. While my team responded positively, corporate organizational culture was forced to react by the polarizing nature of the topic in our society.

Human Resources offices around the country compel associates to accept and not question. But in facing my issue head on, leaving no stone unturned, explaining what was happening and seeking to provide answers where I could, I found the team united around me in the workplace. I was proud of how it was handled and speak to it today on stage.

Summer's idea of how I could visit with my clients about my transition was as genuine and authentic as it could be coming from me. Once that was decided, my calendar filled up with planning and appointments. I had vacation saved up for my normal annual December vacation and would combine it with medical leave. I figured that I would be out of the field with vacation and short term disability most of November and December.

For years, I had seen my clients every two weeks. I had great access to the doctors and was attentive to the time they gave me whenever I arrived, planned or unplanned. Many of the providers I would see over the course of the next six weeks I had known for years, some for the duration my twenty-four year career with this current division of the company. I would be relieved to tell many of them my intention for the rest of my life, because I knew they had to have been wondering "What the hell is going on with him?" From the perspective of someone that I had conducted business with, it would have been a lot of change in a short amount of time. This revelation would provide some answers, and would make sense as the culmination of what they had seen progressing every few weeks for the last two years. An explanation was coming. An explanation, that up to this point, I would have been incapable of delivering.

The first order of business was business. I represented an anticoagulant medication that was used for the treatment of deep vein thrombosis, pulmonary embolism, or stroke prevention in patients with atrial fibrillation. The usage of this class of medication is important and life-saving. Any information, new or as a reminder, was vital to our patients. We covered what we needed to cover in our encounters and as usual, the providers made it clear when their time was at an end. "Could

I have a moment of your time in the office to discuss something with you?" I would ask. I was never turned down. Not once. My relationships with my clients had been so authentic that what I was asking over and above my normal visit immediately moved to the Important Category. Their attentiveness was special, and it was here that I had began to have a paradigm shift in my belief system about what most people care about and want for others.

Doctors are usually great at taking or delivering serious information. They turn on the listening skills so that they understand what is being conveyed. "What's going on?" became the normal opener, once behind closed office doors.

"I want to let you know that I'm going to take some time out of the field in November and December. I'm going to transition and when I come back after the first of the year, I'll be a woman." Just like that. Sometimes I said "a girl." Responses ranging from "No shit?" "Let me hug you," to "I have several patients that have done that" followed my revelation.

The physicians, men and women, whom I had known for a long time were open and candid with me during our regular visits. We would talk money, vacation, and politics. I had been allowed into their private lives. Now, I was scared of the reactions that I might experience. It was during these visits where the strongest personalities, political views, and opinions were all laid on the altar of compassion and acceptance. The most masculine men knew that it must have been a difficult decision based simply on how I had lived my life to this point. The reactions conveying their feelings and acceptance were gifts to me. The toughest to inform were the strong female physicians roughly my age. They were where I wanted to be as soon as I could join them—a strong successful woman living her best life with meaning and purpose. These women had gone to medical school when they were outnumbered in their classes by men and were now excelling in their careers. As I shared my intention to transition, they showed more kindness than I could've possibly expected.

For the next six weeks, my ideas of how this would play out were constantly turned upside down and my predictions of how my clients would react proved to be wrong many times, humbling me. I was surprised, but pleasantly, with the indifference some displayed. Many, as we would discuss later, had patients in their practice who had transitioned. My choice wasn't as uncommon as I had initially believed. I simply didn't know anyone to relate with on a subject that had privately consumed me for years. What a relief. I didn't feel so different.

These experiences solidified my belief that people genuinely want the best for each other. We are consumed with our own lives at home and in our places of business. Worrying about the lives of others can be a distraction to the miserable. I found them to be small in number.

I'LL MAKE YOU PRETTY

I had no interest in making a transition without being able to be identified as the woman who I had seen staring back at me from the mirror. For me to be in alignment with her, I would need to feel what she would feel and look like what I had seen in the mirror. We would eventually occupy the same space, but there was work needed to make that happen. What I had envisioned for the future set the bar high. That meant hormone treatment to effect feminization at the physical level, and to relieve the stress of a forthcoming gender transition.

I'd spent decades with daily access to the best advice the medical community could offer on almost any medical treatment one could consider for life-changing care. But I was at a dead end when it came to any informed advice from my circle regarding the subject of gender.

Miranda, my therapist, gave me two names to consider connecting with for the hormone therapy. The first option didn't actually work in the field and was a dead end. The next option was really unique. He had started treating patients after his own daughter desired to gender transition and couldn't find the informed care that would be needed as she pushed forward with her change. Mark recognized the unmet need and developed a soft spot and a heart for those who needed the guidance that was seriously lacking in the local community. We hit it off immediately.

I wasn't his typical gender patient. I was personally and professionally successful, with no confusion about my goals. I had done my research, wanted some answers, and had years of familiarity with the healthcare system. I knew the risks of HRT and wanted to push forward with the best course of action for my situation. I was open to learning and understanding as much as possible from his experience. We would end up having excellent conversations as my treatment progressed. As I researched and shared my findings, the exchange of information with Mark informed him of the anecdotal evidence from larger patient bases than he would see locally.

We initiated my regimen using a "start low, go slow" approach with oral estradiol. I would work up over time to higher dosages and later add progesterone to my regimen. This would give me the physical and emotional changes I desired, and allow me to make progress at a pace that pushed me to be aggressively patient. I would be aggressive where I had control with what I could do to make the physical changes I desired, and patiently wait for the effects of the HRT to manifest.

It is important to note that the time it would take me to transition from living as guy to a girl was intentionally meant to be short. I clearly understood the topics of biology and gender identity. This had nothing to do with biology. This had everything to do with my intention to live in alignment with how I wanted to experience the rest of my life. In thought, and physically. To be successful, I needed to be identified and live as woman. Period. What it would do, hopefully, is put an end to decades of me chasing the next goal or hobby, mastering it, and still feeling unfulfilled. I would move onto the next challenge and start the process over again. I'd been searching for the best version of myself and not finding it. I would make the transition short and move on. I had no intention of living in the identity of "trans" for any longer than it took me to make the transition to living as a woman.

It would take some talent and experience to transform me physically … mostly in my face. Of course, I wanted to look like a supermodel fitness babe. In my dreams. God made some beautiful creatures when snatching Adam's rib. But no matter what shape my body would end up taking, it was my face I needed to change most. There is no normal when it comes to body shapes. I've been a professional stylist for years now. Coaching women to accept this fact is one of my favorite aspects of that role.

I would choose one of two options. The first was a total facial reconstruction with a transition specialist in San Fransisco known worldwide for his ability to take a male face and reshape it into an attractive feminine presentation. He had the appealing advantage of having attended the University of Oklahoma School of Medicine (sarcasm). His procedure would consist primarily of an aggressive skeletal breakdown of the prominent male bone structure, then rebuilding it to a softer, identifiably feminine shape. His work was amazing. I had an acquaintance that was a patient and her results were beautiful.

My other option was a woman who had recently moved into the Oklahoma City medical community. I had received a referral from a consultant who had toured her medical facility and suggested I investigate the potential she had to help me. A graduate from the University of Florida with both medical and dental degrees, Courtney Caplin was selected for a prestigious fellowship focused on facial, breast, and body procedures. And she was really young. She excelled in her field, was driven, and had a heart for changing lives. This woman was unique and gifted.

I called both to begin my information gathering.

These phone calls weren't easy to make, regardless of my "enthusiasm" for making this change. I had not struggled with gender identity. I had buried it under multiple layers of life experience as a successful man. I was exhausted after every accomplishment. I would rest, then sign up for achieving the next goal that grabbed my attention. For the last seventeen years, I typically dragged my wife into the repeated process, selling her on why the next pursuit made sense. After our trip to San Antonio, the inevitability of this transition was acknowledged and she became part of the decision-making process and the consults. I didn't have to drag her, but she wasn't joyful about the circumstances.

The OU grad would do exactly as expected. The approach would be aggressive. Confident of success, I set a tentative date for the consultation.

Next up was Dr. Caplin. With me being local, the initial consult was scheduled easily.

It came shortly after our trip to the Alamo. Summer and I arrived, checked in, were made comfortable, and treated like gold. Dr. Caplin had joined the practice to work with her husband, Dr. Erik Nuveen, a well-known plastic surgeon in Oklahoma City. The staff told me he loved working on noses. Dr. Caplin brought a lot of Florida with her—she had blanketed the office with inviting pink accents and branding. The business was growing. Fast.

Called by the nurse and taken to an exam room, we waited for the doctor to arrive. Having a strong sense of self-awareness, I realized that this process was the most remarkable thing I had taken on in my life. I appreciated the absurdity of the moment. The Harley-riding, masculine husband was going to trade in the American Dream, transition to a woman, and dive headfirst into one of the most polarizing actions being played out in the culture and political landscape.

Dr. Caplin gave a tiny knock, entered, and greeted me and Summer. She was so kind about bridging into the subject we were there to talk about that I'm not even sure how we found ourselves discussing our options. Pulling up the rolling stool that every doctor has in every room, she had me sit down face to face with her. I mentioned the aggressive procedure in San Francisco to her. She studied my face and responded, "You don't need all that. Your shape is in the normal female range for face shape." Thinking like an artist with a fresh canvas, she knew immediately how she would proceed. She began, "I'm going to smooth your brow ridge; men have a more prominent brow than women. I will reduce yours as well. I'll give you a brow lift during the process to show off your beautiful eyes. We will use a filler that will last for quite a long time for cheekbone prominence and to fill your temple area. This will give the area a more rounded, youthful, and feminine appearance."

Self-assured, she continued, "I will perform a four-millimeter lip lift to shape your lips, and then incrementally fill them over several visits to the desired shape before we are done. You'll need to pick what kind of nose you want so we can do that, too. I will finish your face with a controlled resurfacing. You'll be smooth, it will remove years of damage, and you'll look fifteen years younger."

I was silent. I decided to put my cards on the table. I had to say something because she'd just delivered a clear and deliberate plan of action. "I work every day in the Oklahoma City medical community. Over two hundred of your colleagues will see your work on display when I come through the door. They will want to know who did the work on my face when I return to the field. What about that?"

She looked at me and, not missing a beat, responded, "Bring it. I'll make you pretty."

I knew she could deliver on that statement. "Okay! Let's pick some boobs!" I clapped my hands together, signifying the decision was made to move forward with Dr. Caplin, and now it was time to pick the size and type of implants I would choose to have her put in place.

There is a top made for "trying on" different implant sizes in the mirror. I slipped it on and the first pair were slid in for our review. "Next," I said. The second, third, and fourth received the same reaction.

The look that I wanted to create for myself wasn't that difficult to imagine. I wanted attractive breasts. I wanted them noticed, but not enormous. The issue with the standard sizes was that they were being placed on a body that had a muscular chest and more importantly, a broad shoulder structure. We made a significant move up in implant volume and at last started making progress. We needed them to look "normal" and fit the body, regardless of what size we settled on. Summer had quietly observed the process taking place. She had been reserved in the conversation regarding my face, which is understandable. Neither of us knew what it would take to deliver the finished product from the neck up. When I had my vision of the physical features I wanted to manifest for myself with this transformation, I was relying on Dr. Caplin to create the pretty face with her talent and skill. But from the neck down, it was the three of us with opinions and "Everybody loves boobs," as Summer had said before.

I had a tiny waist. I'd maintained my fitness well over the last decade. Triathlon racing was in the past, but maintaining my health had never stopped being a priority. We continued going up in the size of the implants, quickly increasing until we were close, and then we slowed down and started sharing our thoughts. I said something along the lines of "go big or go home." That fell flat, but we finally got to the last two pairs as realistic options. The sizing fell in range to give the desired shape on the outside edge, with the perfect distance between the two implants in the middle. We all wanted perfect cleavage. No need to push them together or leave a wide gap in between the two. After the next size up was noticeably too large, I felt confident with the sizing we would take to the procedure.

Dr. Caplin had been a pleasure. We all felt sure about where we were headed together to make this change happen. She handed us off to her assistant to schedule the date and to discuss the financial cost of a new physical identity. It damn sure wasn't going to be cheap.

Team Andrea had just signed its first superstar in Courtney Caplin.

IT NEVER WAS TOXIC

With Dr. Caplin confident in the outcome of a physical transition, my last hurdle was cleared. In October, I filed the court papers to legally change my name from David Andrew to Andrea Leigh, the name Summer and I had chosen together on our trip to San Antonio. I incurred several trips to the courthouse for filings, notifying and declaring my intention for the public record, before I appeared before the judge. Summer, Mason, and I appeared in court together. I was dressed in a navy dress with white polka dots and white pumps. The judge called us to appear in front of the bench and asked why I was changing my name. "Because I intend to live the rest of my life as a woman and want a name that is appropriate," I responded. He was pleasant. He tapped his gavel and declared, "Approved."

Andrea Leigh was born.

We gathered our things, made multiple "originals" of the court documents at the courthouse, and headed for a new driver's license. Within hours, I was official within the eyes of the law. Trips to the Social Security Administration, our banking institutions, and calls to the human resources department over the following weeks seemed like little bumps on the road to one of the biggest changes one could undertake.

I needed to pay for that change. It was going to be fucking expensive. I looked at all the possibilities. I had money, assets, no debt, and a sizable income. The funds I needed would combine fast enough that by the time payment was due, I would have most of it. But I wouldn't start life as Andrea with a debt burden. In the back of my mind, I didn't want to tie my wife financially to the loss of her husband. I knew what I needed to do to cover the rest. It was an easy decision.

I loved my motorcycles. All of them. I had previously purchased a BMW R1200RS. A sport touring model with the historically dependable boxer engine, it was sporty, powerful, and beautiful, and painted BMW-logo blue and ecru. It was easily the most high-tech bike I had ever owned or ridden. The year before, Summer and I had decided to take it to Kansas City to visit cousins. We geared up in all of our safety gear, packed all the clothes we would need for a few days, and headed north on the Oklahoma backroads towards Kansas.

On what turned into one of the hottest days of the summer, we learned fast how difficult it was to stay cool on the hot asphalt. No matter how fast we rode, or how much we drank, we were miserable. In constant communication through our helmet intercoms, we decided to exit the state highway and hit the interstate. Getting off the black asphalt, and doing over 80 mph, we blew into Kansas City feeling better as the trip wound down. The last leg of the trip home was much more pleasant and the two of us chalked up another cool experience together.

Then there was the Harley. We would ride into the city, stop at the Harley-Davidson dealer for hot dogs, and fashion shop on Saturday afternoons. We loved riding together. But unfortunately, the 2013 Street Glide was horribly uncomfortable for Summer as the passenger. I would wince as we hit bumps in the road, knowing that they were multiplied for her on the back. So I upgraded the Harley by trading up to a 2017 Ultra Limited. New engine, performance exhaust and audio, with multiple ways to configure the seating, the bike was built for comfort and any length of trip we desired.

And then there was the dirt bike. I hadn't taken it anywhere outside of our pasture in ages. But seeing the beefiness of the motocross bike sitting in the shop on its stand was a reminder of some pretty cool experiences in my life.

Yet I loved who I was becoming more than I did those bikes. I knew the risks of motorcycles. I had ridden from the age of five. I had worn all the safety gear for most of my rides, and enjoyed those bikes safely over the last six years. Moving forward with a physical reconstruction of myself with the purpose and intent to be beautiful pushed me over the limit of what I was comfortable with. I was getting a new face and body.

I wasn't risking them for the enjoyment, thrill, and occasional surge of adrenaline.

A motocross bike, a BMW 1200, and a Harley-Davidson Screaming Eagle sat in the garage with posters of champions, calendars of swimsuit models next to choppers, and pictures of the bikes themselves. It was masculinity.

It never was toxic. It was muscle, strength, toughness, sturdiness, assertiveness, and boldness. That was me taking on long-distance triathlon. It was learning to graze cattle and firing my AR-15s at the range. It had nothing to do with being a man. It had to do with living. Being a woman wouldn't slow me down.

I could let the bikes go. I wanted to live and experience what was speeding down the road. Getting closer and closer every day. *That* would be living.

ANDREA, WE HAVE A PROBLEM

Summer and I went out for a nice dinner on our anniversary, one week before the scheduled procedure. Subdued because of an impending change in the nature of our relationship, we were also exhausted. Absolutely exhausted. For two years, either one or both of us had been riding a roller coaster of emotions. It had been two years since Batman and Wonder Woman had laughed until the tears rolled. We had revealed our most inner thoughts and secrets, asked questions of each other that we had always wondered about, and received answers.

The last two years had been quite a ride for me. Locking into the security of our marriage, I began a journey of self-discovery. A discovery that some would call a nightmare. I always thought my transition was going to be short. I thought it would be the time it took to heal and return to work. I realized that meant my transition was almost over and I would soon live into who I was to become, the very next week.

For the same two years, after slipping and falling in the mud, Summer had battled with a herniated disc, regular injections to alleviate the pain in her back, and multiple appointments for physical therapy. As she recovered from her back injury and SI joint displacement, she injured herself in an accident, resulting in an extreme case of frozen shoulder. Recovering again after shoulder surgery, she began her journey into the world of Pilates. The stabilization of her body that the system offered gave her the most relief she'd had in years. Her gift of teaching, previously seen in ballet, was later transferred to her as a gifted Pilates instructor. She was just beginning that journey as we "celebrated" our life together.

As we sat in the booth, under the lights, against the wall, we were spent. "Do you want to move?" I asked. I'd surprised myself with the question. It didn't seem like a surprise to her.

"Yes," she responded instantly. There. It was done. We both knew it was the right thing for us.

The country life, designing the systems of the ranch, and seven years of daily solitude after work and our activities, had given us a tremendous experience. We felt enormous gratitude for the work of farm and ranch producers everywhere that bring food to our table. We never wasted anything. We loved our land, the cattle, the rest of the animals, the wide open spaces, but we were exhausted. Our lives had taken a toll on us over the last two years and we weren't so naïve as to believe that it would get emotionally easier. The work of the ranch left our cups empty, and there was no way to fill them up. Summer began the search within days. It was time to experience something a bit more relaxing. We would move back to Oklahoma City. It was where I was from, my parents still lived there, and it was where I worked. It would be closer for Summer's Pilates instruction. We were relieved.

A quick referral and a meeting with a new agent, who became a good friend, led us to begin the search process within days. The rise of property values, especially the size of ours, had skyrocketed. We would be in the market for a new home that neither of us thought was attainable when we were younger.

***

Some time after our decision to sell the property, I received a call from the surgery center saying they needed the results of a pre-op EKG. This was a surprise to me, but not unusual. I worked in cardiology and I knew getting this scheduled within a week would be problematic. I felt sick. Luckily, I was able to schedule a routine EKG in the office of my primary care provider. Easy peasy. Until the results showed a tiny abnormality.

"We have an issue. There is a small rhythm abnormality in your test. I want a cardiologist to conduct a test and review it again." My doctor and friend was telling me this as I was buttoning my shirt. Not tiny enough for him to sign his approval for surgery.

This was my field of work. I took it seriously just hearing the news. I was nervous, for my health.

I was able to schedule a second EKG with a doctor with whom I had been conducting business. The abnormality was small, and doctor deemed it insignificant, considering I never had symptoms under times of stress or exertion, such as triathlon and running. Whew. We were still on schedule.

Since my surgery was scheduled two days before the holiday, we had Thanksgiving dinner early. Always grateful for our blessings, Summer, Mason, and I were alone, settling in for what would be two months of seclusion. We would get to watch a lot of football.

DEADPOOL

I needed to be at the surgery center at 5:30 a.m. It was dark, and cold that morning. Since we lived fifty miles from the surgery center, we packed and planned for an overnight stay. Staying for observation was going to the best for everyone. With no complications, I would be released to recover at home the following day.

Summer and I were met at the door by one of the nurses. We anxiously waited in silence for a couple of minutes in the quiet waiting room while an exam room was being readied. I didn't have to wait long. I was taken to pre-op to change into a surgical gown, then taken to another room, where I was asked to wait for the rest of the staff and Dr. Caplin. My feelings were similar to nervous race energy—the energy that I felt before a triathlon or now, walking onto the stage. I was nervous because so much preparation had been made and this was a one-time deal. There would be no do-over.

Courtney Caplin walked into the room, confident, smiling, and ready to put her skill to the test. She grabbed a surgical marker, pulled out the stool again, sat down, and started to create what would be the map to get me to the next destination on my journey. Marking the lines on my face, some solid, others dotted, she created the template for what would be an amazing transformation. She asked me and Summer, "Do you have any questions or concerns?" We shook our heads from side to side. We didn't. Dr. Caplin told Summer that the procedure would take four to five hours. I was then taken to the surgical center and given general anesthesia. I started the familiar countdown from one hundred and was out. Summer waited alone for hours during surgery. We don't talk about it much, but the gut-wrenching feelings Summer experienced are hard for her to describe to anyone.

The first task at hand was my breast augmentation. During the fitting, not having transitioned completely, the guy in me had kept repeating "go big or go home." I had told my best friend that I would "get boobs you'll be proud of" when I described what would take place in the surgery. I had chosen a size of implant that would be appropriate to my frame and shoulder width. A smaller implant would not have been enough to give me an obviously feminine appearance and keep the look I had envisioned for myself. Dr. Nuveen told me later how he felt taking on the challenge of placing them during the procedure. "I thought we would never get those in," he said. Dr. Caplin had responded, "Oh, we are getting them in." While it was the most uncomfortable part of my recovery, having nice breasts is pretty cool from where I now stand.

The uniqueness of my situation before and after is that I was and am still open with my friends, colleagues, and family when talking about the procedure. It was not lost on me that many people would be impacted in various ways by what I would undergo and who I would physically become. Who I was at the core of my being would not change, but the package I was contained in would align with what I envisioned and how I wanted to live moving forward. They would lose a huge part of how they related to me. Guy to girl, masculine to feminine, bald to blonde, son to daughter, firearms to fashionista (I still like the guns).

I didn't expect an understanding of what I was doing. I was just hoping for the acceptance of my decision. I have been full of gratitude in the years since for that acceptance. I'm proud of having been open, honest, and a refreshing alternative to what is considered stereotypical in a gender transition.

The facial reconstruction followed the breast augmentation. It was extensive and aggressive in the amount of work done in one procedure. Dr. Caplin made an incision that ran from temple to temple over my forehead. My face was "peeled down," and my brow ridge was ground down to a more smooth, feminine appearance. It was here that I received my "free bonus" procedure. My older cousins had brutalized me when we were young. Several years younger, I wanted nothing more than to keep up with them. As a three-year-old, I was dragged around in the red wagon, to be run into walls and corners of the car, and loaded into the back of moving station wagons. All this took a toll on my skull. Many sets of stitches later, little and not-so-little bumps had resulted, causing my hats to fit crooked my whole life. During prep, I had asked Dr. Caplin a question that began with, "Oh by the way, these bumps here…" I awoke later to a forehead as smooth as a bowling ball.

Dr. Caplin had inquired beforehand about what kind of nose I would like to have created. I had picked out and saved images of models with beautiful noses to show her at the time. But when pressed, I said, "I'll take your nose."

"Then I will have Dr. Nuveen do your nose, since he did mine," she answered.

He did an amazing job. My new nose was smaller, less bulbous, and more "pointy." I had asked for his wife's nose and he accommodated. I never have compared our noses since the surgery, but he delivered a fantastic rebuild inside and out. It would take almost a year to fit to the new frame underneath, but I noticed my ability to breathe better immediately upon waking from surgery.

Filler was placed in the cheekbone area and around my temples. Months later, my face noticeably rounder and more feminine, I was pleased we didn't choose to go with skeletal restructuring. I just did not need the aggressiveness to get what I wanted.

After the four-millimeter lip lift to bring the upper lip closer to the nose, the first of five lip injections closed out the creation of my favorite part of my new face. An aggressive laser resurfacing took years of sun damage off. My face would be smooth as a baby's as it healed over the next month.

After five hours, I was wheeled to recovery for monitoring. Dr. Nuveen visited Summer in the waiting room. "She is out of surgery. It went well, and she's in recovery. Here are two prescriptions that you need to get filled. She will need these afterwards." Summer thought to herself, *I could've done this while I was waiting. Now I need to get this done before she wakes up.* It took her multiple stops to get the prescriptions filled, trekking all over a part of town that she wasn't familiar with. She made it back before I woke and waited in the private room where we would stay the night.

Dr. Nuveen found Summer on the sofa waiting for an update. I was right behind him, tightly wrapped with bandages around my head, forehead to chin and front to back. The wrappings gave me a "squishy-faced" look. Still under the effects of general anesthesia and shivering terribly, I was brought by wheelchair to the room. Summer began to sweat, got nauseous, and went into the bathroom. Coming out after a couple of minutes, she told the nurse, "I tend to faint and I am not feeling very good." She immediately went down in a heap. Dr. Nuveen was still on hand and helped get her to the couch. Recovering from the fainting spell to pull off one of the best acting jobs in the world, she rocked her wedding vows perfectly over the next few days and weeks to help me recover from husband to wife.

For the remainder of the day, I was given medications for inflammation, pain relief, and antibiotics. Every two hours this regimen was followed. I recovered enough from the procedure to get up, go to the restroom, and look in the mirror. If I had thought that the image of the beautiful woman would be staring back at me, it would've been the cruelest joke in history. I looked as if I had been beaten by a baseball bat. Bruised, burned, swollen, with new nose, lips, forehead, and cheeks, all I had undergone had taken me leaps backwards in appearance. Summer said, "You look like Deadpool!" and laughed out loud. She tickled herself with that one. She was recovering from the initial shock and powering through my post op recovery. Our sense of humor with each other is one of our marriage's superpowers.

Dr. Caplin came into the room to check my progress before leaving for the day. She leaned in real close to review the results and said, "Beautiful. Just looks beautiful."

By the evening, Summer needed some help with my care. She called my sister Erin, who was in town with my parents for the Thanksgiving holidays, to see if she would spend the night with us at the surgery center. Erin reminded her that I had asked for no visitors. Summer knew that, but told her that it had been my desire to not upset my parents further, especially with my appearance. My sister arrived after dark and in the cold, and joined us for the rest of the evening, alternating caring for me with Summer. She hadn't known what to expect and upon seeing me bandaged, exclaimed, "Oh wow! Boobs! I don't think I realized the extent of the procedure." She never said another thing about the procedure to me, or reacted to my appearance at all.

In the morning, I was released by Dr. Caplin, loaded into the car, and we headed back to the ranch. After an uncomfortable emergency bathroom break, we arrived at the house and I immediately went to the bedroom for recovery. Having celebrated Thanksgiving the previous week, Summer had already prepared some of our favorite meals for us to have during this time. Rigatoni with meat sauce and cheese was our meal the day after we returned home. My face may have looked like it was used for batting practice, but I would eat her Spicy Rigatoni through those new lips anytime.

I established a daily routine that included keeping my face moisturized and clean. Showering and washing the ointment off my burned face would cause the old skin to slough off, as desired. I would pat my face dry, reapply the ointment, and go another day. Summer was truly dealing with Deadpool, as she continued referring to me in those first few days.

If all of this sounds painful, it wasn't. The toughest part of the recovery was having the implants positioned under my pec muscle. I was and still am fairly athletic. Remaining disciplined for the best possible outcome meant adjusting my future workouts to a new routine. Using my chest for any exertion at all was uncomfortable, to say the least. Breast augmentation is usually a three- to six-month recovery to a new normal. Mine would take every bit of six. I couldn't shave my face for three weeks, drive the car with implants, and I never considered taking my Deadpool face public. We were perfectly compliant. Nothing was going to keep the results from being anything but stellar if Summer and I had anything to do with it.

We skipped seeing our families for the Christmas and New Year's holidays, our favorite time of the year. My face would need three weeks before it was ready for public broadcasting.

We did venture out once between the procedure and Christmas, when Summer found a house for us to consider purchasing after our decision to move back to Oklahoma City. Covered in a long coat, scarf, and with a bandana around my bandaged head, I left the ranch to meet a good friend and realtor, Vanessa, for the showing. Backing up to a small lake at the edge of Oklahoma City, the home had a beautiful view of the water and was about twenty minutes from my parents' house. We said "yes" and traded the view of our pasture and cattle for one that had us overlooking the water, ducks, and geese year-round. We would exchange the country life for a return to the city. It would be a good move. But for a few more weeks in December, I stayed inside to continue my recovery. I had a couple of weeks left of privacy. It was almost time to return to work.

2019 OKLAHOMA SOONERS
BIG 12 CHAMPIONS
12 - 2

WE'RE ALL WEIRD

I must've stood in the closet for hours as the time to go back into the field as Andrea, the Health and Science Specialist, for the first time approached. I knew with the way I'd invited my clients and their staffs into the transition process, my return to a regular appointment schedule would be generating some interest in the community.

I didn't know a single person who had transitioned genders and I believed that I could give hundreds of others something to experience with me. Since it was also a professional transition, I realized it would have a ripple effect. There was a possibility of my presence simply being disruptive to office productivity, if the water cooler talk expanded beyond the water cooler. I'd made sure that I filled those initial days back in the field with appointments to see clients personally vested and genuinely supportive of my choice. I couldn't wait to return to those offices as Andrea. I was authentically myself, aligned on the inside and out, and knew it would only get better from this point.

Oklahoma City is a "small" big city. The medical community is impressive and the talent in the industry around it, including pharmaceutical, medical device, and supply companies, are well known to each other on an individual level. I knew I was a topic, I just didn't want to be seen as a lesson to anyone struggling with life-altering choices to play it safe and say "No."

I chose a nice, black plaid skirt, a black turtleneck sweater, black tights, and tall black boots. Hair held off my face by a headband, I took some pictures like a kid for the first day of school. I followed the routine that had served me for years that first morning. I showered, did my makeup, and had a great breakfast of eggs, sausage, and oatmeal. Pouring myself two containers of coffee, I went to the car, which was already loaded with my iPad and visuals. I backed down the drive with Summer seeing me off as usual.

I headed straight to the offices where I had developed long relationships over many years. The reception was everything I had visualized when my transition process started three months before. They were waiting, interested, and kind. I had healed nicely over the last six weeks. I was happy with the results and the reception in the offices. They were pleased for me, and relieved that I "turned out okay." None of my clients had known what to expect upon my return.

Offices across the city were ready because I had shared my life with them when I didn't have to be open. Both before and after my return to the field, many were struck by my willingness to share about the process. I believe that my sharing the journey with my clients from the start was important to my story; that without being authentic and vulnerable, the confidence in the path I'm taking now, years later, might not have been so strong. What a lesson for others to consider when struggling with something so personal and tightly held.

Heart racing at every office I entered, I walked to the desk and handed them my card as usual. The receptionist would pick up the phone to call back to the nurses' station, hang up, and say, "They are waiting for you," with a smile. The reception was wonderful. Time after time, I was given approval to see the providers and received nothing but graciousness at every turn. As a liaison between the company and the providers using our medications, we were stuck with each other. They were part of the process.

I had met some of these physicians during their residency and seen their practices grow and careers blossom. The relationships we built were genuine and offered much opportunity to discuss what I had done physically to transition. They were fascinated with the outcome.

"You look amazing."

"She did an amazing job."

"You have to give me her name." This was what I was hoping to hear. I'd been confident this would happen. I described the procedure multiple times a day.

I was thrilled with the results of the reconstruction, and I was still healing. My face was puffy and swollen. It would take a year for my nose to form to the reconstructed frame, my breasts to look natural. Fillers in my face would draw collagen to enhance my cheekbones for months, and I still had four more incremental treatments ahead to fill my lips. I was so concerned about the drooping right eyelid from the initial botox treatment that I was taking eyedrops to relax the muscle around the eyelid and therefore lift the lid to look mostly normal. Some botox had migrated with all the swelling from surgery, and the effect lasted a few weeks. But a few days after I returned to the field, the effect had dissipated. I was happier than I had ever been with me. I loved the new me.

***

But damn, it was cold and winter coats were on the shopping list. Fall-Winter fashion offers some real opportunity for individual expression. Skirts with matching jackets or coats called to my sensibilities, and I continually added to my wardrobe for the cold weather that I had yet to experience as a woman. I was easily the most chic pharma representative in the Oklahoma City area. I hit the local White House Black Market boutique whenever I had a break in my schedule. I had built an affinity for the brand due to its chic fashion, price points, and quality of apparel. A loyalty developed for the brand due to the reception I received during the awkward time of transition. The manager and I had forged a friendship that continues to this day. She was a career retail industry professional who would play a pivotal role in my future.

I scoured the current styles and, and clothing websites of all kinds of designers, and I knew the products as well as I understood any antidepressants, blood pressure medications, or the anticoagulant I currently represented. The associates met me with enthusiasm when I dropped in to see if any new styles had arrived. Ginger Short, a mother of three, was and continues to be one of the top salespeople I have ever had the pleasure of working with, in any field, over the course of my sales career. Not quite five feet tall, she towered over the store in her knowledge and control of her products and clients. She told me the truth about my appearance in the styles we took to the fitting area. I trusted her and the rest of the staff to care for me as I built out a professional wardrobe for a position where appearance and professionalism was highly regarded.

For years, my employer sat at the top of the list as one of the most respected and professional healthcare companies in the industry. I was going to make sure I did my part with my fashion sense and uphold the standard. Pencil skirts, sweaters, and suiting filled the closet in no time. It was not long after my return to the field that my access to the physicians opened up significantly compared to other business partners in the industry. I felt more confident and aligned with who I was than at any other time in my life. It translated to a more focused and confident partner for the physician and her staff. With the explosive growth of managed healthcare over the last twenty years, the job wasn't only about selling product features and benefits anymore. It was about partnering with the healthcare team to ensure access to the medications patients needed. I was required to know more about formulary status on a daily basis than the studies that had been done for years. And I was doing that better than at any other time in my career.

The first months after my return were a joy. There were no surprises with my appearance. I repeatedly met wonderful responses of acceptance and the pleasant reinforcement that Dr. Caplin was an amazing surgeon who delivered on her promise. I was continuing to heal and turning out okay. Well, better than okay.

Catering pies into one of my favorite clinics a few weeks after my return, I visited with the doctors and the clinic staff about anticoagulation. As the number of staff dwindled, I was left with one of my clients. We were side by side looking at patients in the waiting room. Watching a noticeably troubled man that had been watching me, the doctor shook his head in frustration. I commented, "He's so weird," then realized what I had just said. We slowly turned to face each other. "That was an interesting thing for me to say."

He didn't miss a beat. "We are all weird." It was a powerful statement that still resonates with me.

The offices that I was unable to have conversations with before the transition struggled with what amounted to a sudden change in appearance in those initial encounters. Right up until the moment that they walked in for those breakfast or lunch appointments, the company representative had been a guy. Walking into the break room to share some words over a meal, they were met by a massive, unexpected change. Anticoagulation guy waiting to visit was suddenly dressed in a chic style. The reaction wasn't always pleasant. They didn't look directly at me, or they took the food and left as soon as possible. It was noticeably uncomfortable for all of us. I was so sure that the route I'd taken to inform my clients ahead of time was the correct one, that I regretted not being able to let everyone know. Unfortunately, there'd been no way to have accomplished that wish. Thankfully, we moved past the awkwardness quickly and our relationships returned to our normal pleasant informative conversations within weeks.

The coordination with my colleagues was seamless. Internal and external business partners were professional, and personally a huge weight was lifted off my mind in not having to deal with the potential drama of a gender change. I showed up every day, went to work as one of the point people these providers depended on, and cemented something that would remain at the core of my being from that point onward. That most of us want the best for ourselves and therefore each other.

In our culture today, most people are so absorbed with their own lives that our perception of the interest they have in us is not based in reality. The gender change wasn't the biggest personal transition in my life. The biggest change was realizing that what holds most of us back from living out our deepest wishes and desires is our perception of what others may or may not be thinking about us. My ensuing life testifies to how fulfilled one can be if one doesn't place one's own personal value on the opinion of others. My self-worth isn't tied to those outcomes anymore. It now has more to do with living a life of abundance and without regret. Today I continue to say "yes" to things that my higher self is drawn towards. This provides me more opportunities and abundance than I could've possibly imagined.

COVID-19

March 12, 2020. I had been working as Andrea for a little over two months when we received the news. We were instructed to leave the field and await further direction. COVID-19 was spreading, fear was rampant, and as representatives, we were in direct contact with frontline healthcare every day. They were busy and it just didn't make business sense to insist on appointments if we were going to be a hindrance to the job at hand. What resulted over the next fifteen months was a massive difference in the way we conducted business all over the world. All of us adapted, suffered, started new endeavors, and succeeded or changed. My experience over the next fifteen months was a combination of all of these.

We had moved from our ranch mere weeks before the stay-at-home routines were put into effect. The ranch had yet to be listed on the market, so we decided to finish the move ourselves. Not something I would advise, but taking the time to do it was not a concern. Multiple truckloads and trips with our stuff got old, but a great group of young men helped us finish off the move by transporting our gym equipment, the baby grand piano, bookcases, and the last heavy items those fifty miles and placing them in our new home.

We listed the ranch and sold it in two weeks. The loss of the beautiful view of the pasture with the cattle grazing every morning stung a little less with a new view of the lake, ducks, and geese from our new back window. We added a pool within six months, and our oasis was complete with the better part of COVID-19 house arrest still in front of us.

While it wasn't really house arrest, that's how I felt about meeting clients virtually instead of in the field. This experience convinced me that preventing an extrovert from going past their curb is not a punishment to make fun of. Eight a.m. meetings, virtual breakfasts and lunches, planning the catering details between virtual sales calls in the morning, and planning the next day's schedule in the afternoon. It really was that boring. Hours on the phone in my home office with a south-facing window. Dang, it was hot in there.

Two months in, I had to do something different. I had been buying up the casual styles now that the office styles were disappearing from current trends. Getting ready every morning as if I was going into the field was paramount. With my face now healing nicely, being camera-ready for those virtual office days gave me some other opportunities. I picked out outfits and accessories for each day. I wore the most appropriately matched shoe to the outfit. My wearing the heels at home amused Summer and Mason, who would hear me clicking from the office through the house for a snack or a bathroom break. But I was intentionally getting my feet more accustomed to being in heels every day.

Another routine began. Unless we had a scheduled team meeting, no provider was getting on to videoconference with me first thing in the morning. Instead, I would head out the door and find a gorgeous spot around the house to take some fashion photos. The house was built of a beautiful stone and had a long drive, a portico from the third garage to the house, and the lake directly behind the property. Well-lit opportunities for a fashion shoot in the outfit of the day abounded. I would ask Summer, "Hey, honey, will you come take a couple of pictures?"

"Tell me when you're ready," she'd answer.

I would roam the property, taking test shots with the lighting and background. Dragging her around while I did that pushed her limits and patience with me. But she endured. Taking the pictures when I was ready and posed, and framing the whole outfit, she worked to bring out the best possible results with my phone. Other times, I would take selfies to get my new tops seen. I would tag the brand, myself, and any other appropriate business that might appreciate the attention. I would then take my place at my adjustable-height swivel chair behind the big wooden desk and start my day with the dogs sitting on the other side of the threshold.

Posting the best photos to Instagram with an appropriate caption ended the first part of my daily routine. I then started the virtual day in the office, coordinating with my partners sitting in their own home offices, while keeping an eye on the likes and comments. We were always careful to balance the need to do our jobs with an understanding of the pressures of the medical community. I believe we handled the situation amazingly well.

This went on for fifteen months, Monday through Friday. Fifteen months with everybody in the world knowing what it was like to be limited in our ability to interact. Personally, I was able to accelerate learning what it meant to be a woman in terms of my appearance and mannerisms, without scrutiny. It was an amazing opportunity for me in both my personal development and professional career. And I would soon say "yes" to more experiences in both areas.

MANSPLAINING CAN BE VALIDATING

I transitioned to live as a woman, be seen as a woman, and be treated as a woman. How should a woman be treated? That depends on who is answering the question, and those answers could fill a library. None will be the same. I have received way more than I expected and everything I bargained for from the men in my world. I mean the ones that cross my path in the process of everyday life. Everything I wanted and more.

Let me share two examples that readily come to mind whenever I am asked about my personal experience with being treated differently under similar circumstances. I had hoped for a little authenticity in my experience. I had no idea how experiences at the car dealership and shipping a package overnight would perfectly accommodate my hopes.

I had been a woman for months. My new iPhone and my new 4Runner were constantly disconnecting from each other. I was at the end of my rope. I was in my vehicle for hours a day on the phone. Constantly being forced to hold it was about to send me through the roof. I actually contemplated buying another vehicle. It was that bad.

I had purchased all of my Toyotas from Jake, the salesman at the dealer. He was familiar with both Andy and Andrea. I took the car to Jake and said, "Fix it." He called back to the service department, specifically to the electronics specialist, and was told to wait at the vehicle. I was in the driver's seat. The tech joined us and sat in the passenger seat. Jake was standing to my left, between me and the open driver's side door. The tech was kind and deferential. He proceeded to give me basic instruction on Bluetooth connection, that it was wireless, how it was to be turned on, and connected. He never listened to what the problem was, making an assumption that I simply didn't know how to connect my phone to the vehicle's audio system. Being a fairly intelligent human and skilled in human connection, I was quite sure he thought the Bluetooth had never been connected. Trying to explain to him multiple times wasn't going to break through his belief system that, because I was a girl, I simply couldn't connect the phone to the vehicle. Each time I tried to clarify, I glanced at Jake shaking his head, smiling with a little more understanding of what was going on.

Seeing it play out in real time brought the two of us so much joy and laughter. The tech couldn't quite understand what we were laughing about. Jake laughed with embarrassment while my laughter produced tears—laughing at the difference I might have experienced had I brought the car in six months prior.

I called Summer and laughed again all the way home. We never did solve the problem. The phone never did stay connected. I finally replaced the phone and had no problems with the latest model, despite my blonde hair.

My second experience was sending some packages through overnight delivery. I had used the same location, receiving help from the same associate, months prior to my transition. On that occasion my box had been taken, forms filled out, and I was told to trust that it would make it to its destination. Done. On this particular day, it seems I must have suddenly lost my knowledge of the how and why one should tape a package. I was educated on the importance of taping it from front to back and once more for reinforcement, and filling out the destination form correctly or suffering costly problems.

I was willing to listen the step by step commentary on the fine art of using a tape gun. It was validating for me. I left with a smile. I laughed at the contrast of experiences. I also understood that it could prove tiresome if one had to deal with that on a regular basis.

I got what I asked for in the experiences. Ladies, I get it.

When Summer asked me, "Have you thought about what kind of woman you want to be?" as we drove to San Antonio, I responded that I hadn't really thought about it at the time. I had never been asked that question. My interaction with the valet provided a great first glimpse. It was obvious how I wanted to be seen physically in terms of my body, fitness, and fashion.

My desire to integrate my physical, mental, and spiritual self was going to take some deep work. Deeper than what a scalpel can find and deliver. I still find the breakthroughs fascinating to pursue today. Many of my new experiences are enlightening because they arise from circumstances having nothing to do with being a woman, per se. And some are so shallow there is no deep work needed. Only a willingness to not be offended, and a great sense of humor.

PHOTOSHOOT AND FASHIONISTA

I was very comfortable with myself now. The most important people in my life, with few exceptions, had accepted the change I had made the previous year. It was a form of gift exchange that we shared with each other, I suppose. I was happy, vulnerable, and had trusted them by being open with my decision. They responded with acceptance for that decision. I was intentional about my self-care, and I knew without a doubt that for my transition to be successful, I had to develop a support network of specialists, friends, and acquaintances that wanted to be part of the story.

The family developed a new normal inside and outside of the home. With the transition behind me, I was now easing into the new life with things everywhere having slowed down. Summer had begun her journey as a healer and was immersed in the process of becoming a certified Pilates instructor.

And things really came together like Dr. Caplin said they would regarding my appearance. Gaby Robinson, an amazing makeup artist, brought me to a level of doing my makeup that made it seem like I had been practicing it for decades. I had my eyebrows professionally mapped and tattooed by Ashtyn Perry, an artist who had moved from Seattle and brought the gift of brow creation with her. Her method had me elated while I still had geometry stenciling all over my face.

In the fashion industry, the retail sector opened back up faster than many other areas of the economy. To stay closed much longer would've crushed it. Even so, it will likely never completely recover from the transfer of customers to online shopping during that time frame.

I had been called a "clotheshorse" by my friends and the sales associates I worked with in the past. I knew my fashion. Always had.

Men's or women's. For the last few years, I had spent a significant amount of time and money investing in a wardrobe overhaul, as one could imagine. I had worked extensively with the local White House Black Market (WHBM) boutique for some time already. The brand has a target market of young to middle aged women with an upscale chic style for work, social, and casual fashion.

The manager, Tonya, who then led the WHBM operations in central Oklahoma, has a character built from a strong upbringing, and an unwavering commitment to the customer who walks through the doors of any establishment whose success she is responsible for. We hit it off immediately. I conducted my business this way in my healthcare career, and was a high-demand customer when I was on the other side of the counter. The boutique treated me like gold. I had found my style for work before the shutdown, and was now becoming more familiar with what I liked to wear casually or socially. I became even better acquainted with the materials and the styles best suited to me as the summer moved on with us still at home.

With COVID-19 and the lockdown continuing, I needed a big goal. I made myself one: a photoshoot. A swimsuit photoshoot. This was bold. We would shoot at the house, by the pool. The plan would cause me to focus on every area for development. Legs, hips, and lean body composition.

I worked out intensely to reshape my body. I had started the process before we left the ranch. High volume core work, more cardio, and a lot less upper body movements. As a guy, I was blessed with arms, chest, and shoulders that would respond well and quickly to strength training. As a girl, nineteen-inch biceps weren't exactly beneficial for someone who didn't desire to have her "guns" admired anymore.

I hired a personal trainer and nutritionist to help me get to another level of fitness. I had trained in bodybuilding methods for decades, but this was going to be a whole new regimen. Erika Barenberg and Amelia Wall of 413 Fitness created a plan for me that reshaped my physique to a feminine shape faster than I could've imagined doing myself. These two were former bodybuilders, and Amelia soon became one of the first female firefighters in the Oklahoma City Fire Department. I had picked the right pair to hold me accountable. Team Andrea now had at least six that contributed significantly to my physical success.

I trained in an unfinished room on our second floor. The elements in Oklahoma could swing between intense heat and bone-chilling cold, and the conditions were accentuated by working out in what amounted to the attic. Setting up my squat rack and olympic weights for barbell squats, hip thrusts, pull-ups, and leg raises, I had all the tools I needed for the job at hand. Dumbbells from five to fifty-five pounds, and a bench for many of the exercises called for, outfitted a gym Rocky Balboa would've high-fived me for training in every day.

I worked out at the end of every virtual workday. I had never trained with the accountability that I felt from Erika and myself. But the toughest thing to overcome was my insane love of ice cream. It was almost my undoing as the photoshoot I had planned grew closer.

For eight months, I had followed the training plan. The increased calories were not so problematic when I was trying to put extra weight on my narrow hips and round out my butt. Yet as the photoshoots grew closer and the weight was slower coming off than it should've been, Erika chastised me like coach ripping a quarterback that continues to throw interceptions in a meaningful game. I was forbidden to eat any more ice cream as the clock wound down on the training plan. "No more free meals until this is over!" she demanded. I knew she was right; I needed to be called out for my lack of adherence to the plan. I hit my peak perfectly, and the photos testified to what is possible with commitment.

***

Outside of my team, I was not interacting with almost anyone since the shutdown. There was no opportunity to connect and get any kind of social connection at all. This was part of why I started posting updates to my new life on Instagram. The decision to use social media was a pivot point that led me down a trajectory I hadn't previously foreseen in thinking about my career path as a woman. I would post fashion pics in the office at the desk, in the backyard by the lake, in front of the bathroom mirror, the garden, or on the driveway. Always in a different outfit. I followed the same routine of a morning cardio workout, getting ready for the day, eating breakfast, and the daily fashion shoot before heading into the home office.

In addition to the daily photoshoot images, I wrote thoughtful, motivational posts that I continue to write today. I tagged the cosmetics I was using. I would sometimes tag the brands of clothing that I wore in the photo posted. I ended most of those posts #fashionista, as I labeled myself. I was happy with the label. I owned it then, and still do.

It had been a year since we had been pulled out of the field due to COVID-19. I was eating five to six times a day like clockwork. My workouts were hard four days a week in the afternoon and I was getting in the best physical shape of my life. On the slower days, those with fewer appointments and conference calls, I went out to the new pool to get sun in the late morning, if the temperatures were agreeable. Mason was writing her first book of poetry, and the three dogs were in the house watching our every move. The hair from two German Shepherds and a shepherd mix could pile up. For each of us, the pandemic offered the opportunity to cultivate aspects of ourselves that would have likely remained undeveloped. I took a writing class and each Saturday for weeks submitted stories from my childhood past. As my writing developed, I realized how the stories we tell ourselves change over time and through reflection. This would become a key point in my personal development coaching in the future.

The virtual workdays continued successfully. But internally, something had to change. I needed connection with people. I took every opportunity to get out for errands or, more times than I want to admit, to see the new styles shipping into the fashion world. There was no slowing down in what was showing up on the runways. Designs had been decided upon and purchased for a year's worth of planned business long before COVID-19 had forced the population to live differently. Sitting at my desk and studying the trends during the day between virtual customers,

I lived in constant anticipation of the current week's arrivals at the national level. With no knowledge of what styles would arrive and when, shipments always felt like Christmas morning to the boutique staff. I would find myself there a short time later passing judgment with my wallet.

Tonya and I developed a nice relationship during this time period. "You should come in and work with us once a week or every other week," she said to me. Tonya continued to follow up on her recruitment efforts several times as the fall and winter continued. The message was clear: I should come work at the boutique in the evening after my virtual workday was finished. "You will get a discount, get to sell products you love, and you can work in a stylist role." She was relentless. Never pushed.

I always shook my head and responded, "Yeah, I'll think about that," or "That would be fun." It was my way of moving the discussion along. I didn't need another job. I needed the people.

BOUGIE

I had finished the 2020 sales year at the top of the rankings again. The customer relationships I had built over years within the medical community paid early dividends for me. Winning as a woman. It was exactly what I had said I would do as Summer and I drove to San Antonio the previous year. Awards were not given out, due to wide-ranging differences with how healthcare communities across the nation dealt with the pandemic. We were now planning the remainder of the 2021 sales year. Other companies in the industry were going back into the field, while ours was conservative with their representatives' safety and conscious of the public perception of being back in offices while the industry was marketing the emergency need for vaccine options to the world. My face was completely healed, and I was way past ready for prime time.

Spring fashion rolled down the runways and into the boutiques around the country. Sitting at the desk in my home office all day every day continued to give me time to become familiar with what was trending. It wasn't odd for me to enlighten boutique management on what was blowing up the internet when I visited.

In March, I took a break from the office, and escaped from the house to see the new styles in person. I found myself in conversation with Tonya. We seemed to always find ourselves naturally standing shoulder to shoulder talking fashion and the industry in general. As we faced the door, watching for customers entering the boutique, she laughed and said, "Lips and hips."

"What did you say?" I asked.

"Lips and hips. Lips and hips face the entry," she answered. The phrase amused me. In the medical environment, it was natural for me to be aware of my surroundings, clinic traffic, and the clock. I would always watch for the physicians to make themselves available without notice. This was no different. No customer should go ungreeted.

I changed the subject. "I think I'll take you up on the offer to come and moonlight as a stylist in the boutique when my day is done or on the weekend."

Tonya squealed in delight. It was a true response of joy. She was beyond thrilled, as was I. This would give me the client interaction I craved. We made plans for me to come back and do the onboarding paperwork before I joined the team in another week or two. I returned home and went back into the office for the rest of the day. Later on, Tonya told me she called upper management that day and told them, "I just hired my replacement."

Returning days later, I felt like I had just gone through a time portal and clocked in again as a seventeen-year-old reporting for my job working in the department store. We went through the federal paperwork to prove my status as a citizen. That was new. I had not done anything like that for over twenty years. The fashion work was an amazing bridge that would end up being more important than I would've ever imagined at the time.

I knew the styles when I joined the industry. What I needed was an education about the differences in fabrics, cuts of jeans, and business processes to remain efficient with staffing, payroll, and servicing the customer in retail locations. The fabrics and denim? I learned that quickly. The inability of some associates to prioritize excellent customer service over tasking what could be done in between, however, escaped me. For the next three years, when I was on location, there would never be any doubt what the priority was.

When I joined the team, the existing staff had found their comfort zones. The assistant manager was talented in creating a visually appealing boutique. She changed the layout of the store almost daily to appeal to the fashion enthusiasts who frequented the business regularly. Other members of the staff were comfortable with filling online orders, helping the customer only if asked, but generally unaware of what the overall goals of the business were for any specific time period.

I was there to be a stylist. I took that seriously from day one. I would come into the boutique for a few hours after my virtual day was over. I conversed with an office of cardiologists about atrial fibrillation during the day, or had lunch with primary care teams discussing vein thrombosis treatment. I continued to prioritize a good workout for my upcoming photoshoot, and then drove to the boutique one night a week to style the ladies of Oklahoma City in the current fashion. With a customer-first mindset, it was easy to impact the fashion business quickly.

I was educating the customer on what to wear, what not to wear, and how to wear the styles that most flattered their body type. I found it fulfilling to see the self-image of the women I assisted change as I adjusted the size of pant or top they were trying on for their next event. The staff watched, learned something, and started to get a little more interested in what might be possible when customers walked through the door. We began moving the needle on sales as well.

Tonya had been a retail professional for years. While I was learning disease states, treatment options, and sales methodology in the biopharma industry, she was learning customer traffic patterns, retail science, and the art of getting the "deeper why" at retail. The "deeper why" was the answer we needed to ensure our customers left with their mission accomplished. She shared her knowledge with me as fast as I could absorb it. I learned swiftly and advanced in my understanding of not only the styling side of the business, but the predictability of human behavior and how to use that knowledge to goal set for a seven-figure fashion business. This became my obsession.

I enjoyed the boutique in the evenings after work. There was a lovely mutual respect with the staff. I felt their genuine affection for me when I arrived for the last few hours of boutique's operations. I had such appreciation for their work in the daily tasks that it takes to run a chic boutique with loyal customers. What they were doing made my job easier as a stylist. Tonya and I made a great team when we worked in the same building. That didn't happen often, though, as she continued to advance in her career and I was about to return to in-person appointments at my day job.

I closed the boutique one evening after a full day's work in the medical field, and failed to process all the waste from the shipment and the last few days of customer returns. I called Tonya on the way home, belatedly remembering the mountain of trash blocking the back door of the boutique. "Oh my gosh, I forgot to process all the waste at the back door. I'm so sorry to leave it for you to deal with tomorrow morning."

"Oh, that's okay, I'll take care of it when I get there," she responded. But the next morning, she flipped out when she saw the size of the mountain of return packaging waiting. Taking care of what I left her, she went home at the end of the day and told Dennis, her husband, how Andrea had left her a huge workload. Very matter-of-factly, he responded, "Andrea doesn't do trash."

Incredulously, she snapped back, "What do you mean, 'Andrea doesn't do trash'?"

"Have you seen those nails?"

He was referring to my long, stiletto fingernails. The discussion was over.

The story came back to me from Tonya herself. I told the rest of the staff about the exchange, and looking at me as if it were no surprise, they said, "Well, that's not you, Andrea."

"What do you mean 'it's not me'?"

"You're too bougie to do trash."

I laughed, embarrassed that it was true, and decided that I would take the trash out. I paused, turned around, and asked, "Would someone go with me and show me how?"

I took out the trash for the first time. It had been months. They loved me for the type of woman I was turning out to be, a work in progress.

***

The summer returned, and we received the news that we were approved to return to in-person visits at clinics and hospitals. I had become a completely different person. Almost two years had passed, and I had healed from the work Dr. Caplin had done. Hormones had a powerful effect on my appearance as well. I was completely at peace in my skin and my new life. I had months of working in fashion as a stylist.

Soon, the team was back in the field, enjoying breakfasts, lunches, and generally having great discussions with the medical staffs. The enthusiasm for returning to work on the front lines was so great, as the crisis wound down, it started to feel similar to twenty years previous, when the industry resembled an entertainment business that sampled medications as a bonus. This time, we were having breakfasts and lunches feeling like the most appreciated partners in the healthcare treatment pathway.

Soon another protocol would change. One that included a vaccine.

PUSHING BACK

The Women's Health Initiative (WHI) study, which partially ended in 2005, found that some of the risks of combined estrogen and progestin hormone replacement therapy (HRT) outweighed some of the benefits for postmenopausal women. The conjugated equine estrogen (CEE), and the combination of CEE and medroxyprogesterone acetate (MPA), were the specific medications used in the study. Research concluded that this arm of the HRT study did not protect as previously thought and, in fact, increased the risks and outweighed some of the possible benefits. This finding had a significant impact on the use of hormone replacement therapy.

After the results were released, showing increased risks associated with hormone therapy, the industry adjusted its marketing strategies, revising their marketing materials and communications to reflect the new understanding of the risks and benefits. Our company also updated labeling and prescribing information for hormone therapy medications to include warnings about the risks identified in the WHI study, such as an increased risk of heart disease, stroke, blood clots, and breast cancer. Overall, our company and other pharmaceutical companies focused on promoting informed decision-making among healthcare providers and patients regarding the use of hormone therapy, emphasizing the importance of individualized treatment decisions based on a thorough understanding of the risks and benefits for each patient.

I was assigned the responsibility for communicating these findings and the updated recommended guidelines to the medical community in my geographic area of responsibility at this time.

***

I had weighed the risks and benefits of hormone related therapy for myself long before COVID-19 became a household word. I had been in the healthcare or pharmaceutical industry for over thirty years. When one is immersed in the medication side of the healthcare industry, it is easy to see a lot of pathologies as nails needing a hammer. I had sold a lot of hammers. Very successfully and with a lot of integrity. I made sure I got objective healthcare and not just what I wanted to hear.

I chose my providers from my history in the industry and by recommendation. I chose an HRT specialist previously unknown to me based on a recommendation and his number of similar cases. I coordinated that with a new primary care physician who had been a client of mine for years. We shared similar thoughts on the balanced use of medical and pharmaceutical treatments. We shared interests in politics, firearms, and we both had small acreages. We had shared resources for the properties before Summer and I sold the ranch and moved back into the city. He would remain objective about my overall health, and manage it while remaining informed on my HRT treatment.

Various vaccines had been brought forward to slow the spread of COVID-19. Months after the vaccine emergency approval for use was announced, the first initiative to increase the number of vaccinated employees at our company was introduced. The vaccine would be available and was being encouraged.

I knew that my personal hormone treatment was not "normal," and carried risks. A biological male doesn't take dosages of female hormones multiple times larger than the dosages included in the WHI and not weigh the risk-benefit ratio. I had a thorough understanding of my choice and moved forward based on discussions with my providers and as suggested in the literature and guidelines for gender transition.

As the usage of the vaccine moved forward inside and outside of the workplace, the benefit of vaccination without the information provided by long-term studies was not worth the risk to me. My own regimen of HRT treatment (different than the regimen studied in the WHI) carried enough risk for a lifetime. Combining the vaccine and my unique HRT regimen was not an option I would consider. When employees were offered vaccinations, I politely declined and accepted a twice a week testing regimen as an alternative. I tested regularly before going into the offices, clinics, and hospitals. Testing for compliance on video eventually transitioned to me self-testing and sending samples via Fed Ex to the lab.

The sales year was well underway, as was a restructuring of one of the sales divisions. One of the other divisions had just been completely terminated after a medication had been denied FDA approval. The displaced employees would find openings within the company or receive lucrative severance packages and find other employment outside. However, the usage of anti-coagulants was increasing due to the risk-benefit ratio and we had an excellent product. My own job was secure.

Until two weeks later, when it was announced that vaccination would be mandated for all employees by Thanksgiving. The first of two doses would be documented, or termination would result. There would be no severance. There was no alternative to vaccination.

I announced my retirement.

COMMITTED

We held a conference call to announce to the team that I would be departing as soon as I received notice of a termination date. I was clear that there were no hard feelings. This was a personal decision that was mine to make, based on principle and on the priorities of the company. I'd had an amazing, long career, though this wasn't the way I envisioned it ending. There were tears all around, and upper management joined the call to show appreciation. After forty-five minutes, I hung up feeling valued for the impact I had made in the business. The respect I had for myself and from others was worth more than any retirement party could've given me.

I received an email saying I would be notified regarding my last day of employment. I continued to work with my clients closely, choosing not share the news of my retirement yet. I also continued to moonlight as a stylist, enjoying the changes in fashion as the seasons turned. I wasn't quite sure which direction I would head. The healthcare industry was consistent at this time in demanding that employees vaccinate, so the healthcare industry wasn't an option.

The email notification I was waiting for never came. I would go through November, Thanksgiving, Black Friday at the boutique, and take my Christmas vacation over the last half of December without further news. The family relaxed with no information forthcoming. We started wondering about lawsuits regarding the mandated usage of the vaccine in those with medical reasons or religious objections.

During this time, another division was surprisingly notified that they would be displaced. These colleagues would be absorbed into a company that was in a partnership with us at the time, if they so desired, and continue under a new employment agreement. Weeks later, we received notice that a restructure of the last division, mine, would be announced in late January. I wondered if this was the reason I hadn't heard anything on a termination date.

If I were to be severed, my tenure would result in a severance package that would equal roughly two years of pay. I would have time to decide what I wanted for my future. Things were looking a little bit brighter. Internally, there were proponents of transitioning the remaining sales teams to a virtual sales or at least a hybrid model. This disturbed me, because the sales teams were already seeing the declining usage of virtual systems within the clinics even before the industry returned to the live office meetings.

When the restructure was announced, it was minimal. Overall, displacement was minor. I was retained. There would be no lucrative severance package. I maintained my role and was reassigned into rural Oklahoma and Texas. My time spent working in the Oklahoma City metropolitan area would be low, and I would be in the car hours a day.

The email I had been waiting for came shortly after the restructure of the final division was announced. I received a date for my termination. Per the vaccination policy, there would be no severance. I could, however, apply for a waiver based on medical reasons or religious grounds. I was relieved. I had already drafted a letter regarding the results of the WHI, my regimen of HRT, and the unknown risk associated with the vaccine approved for emergency use. I submitted it for review.

When I was denied the medical exemption, I was shocked. I was informed there was no evidence of increased risk associated with the vaccination and HRT. Of course, there wasn't. It had not been studied. That was the point. I had sold twenty-seven different compounds over my career, and none had been approved for usage unless the efficacy and safety were clearly evident. I informed one of my providers about the denial, and as I was leaving his office, I turned and said, "You know, wouldn't it just be rich if I were accommodated and could say, 'Thanks, but no thanks'?"

"God has a sense of humor," he said.

I was getting resentful. I was really good at what I did and enjoyed the role. I submitted my request for a waiver a second time with additional data, and was denied a second time.

Good grief. I was now left with the option of seeking a waiver based on religious grounds if I wanted to maintain my position. With my convictions unchanged regarding the risk of combining vaccination and HRT, I sent a request to the compliance department for an exemption based on my personal convictions and what I felt God wanted for me based on my beliefs. I had decided not to submit a request based on some theology I didn't follow to escape termination.

Within days, on a Saturday evening in late January, I received an email from the compliance attorneys in New York: "Your case is being reviewed."

I was winning. When you get Saturday night emails from corporate attorneys, it ain't bad.

My last day as an active colleague, I was in my home office, transferring emails, pictures, and personal documents that I might need in a potential job search off my devices. An email came across the devices. "Your request for an accommodation has been approved."

I cried. I had committed to a course of action, held to principle, and was rewarded.

Two hours later, the phone rang. It was Tonya from the boutique. "Andrea, the reorganization of the company is done. I received a promotion. Would you like a new career in fashion as my replacement?"

"Yes," I responded instantly. *God certainly does have a sense of humor,* I thought. Tonya had no idea what had just happened. I filled her in.

Within a few weeks, while I was vacationing in Santa Fe and walking to the Plaza, the official offer from White House Black Market arrived. I accepted it, hung up the phone, and immediately informed management that I would retire from the pharmaceutical industry. Now it was their turn to be shocked.

An amazing career was over. Another transition awaited.

I had been tested for COVID-19 87 times.

Thanks, but no thanks.

"IT'S AN EXPERIENCE..."

For months, I worked day after day in the boutique. My boutique. The sales results were instantaneous, climbing even with negative traffic growth. I was consumed with driving the business through the previous year's results at a pace greater than almost any other location in the country since before COVID-19. I took full ownership of those results, too.

I posted updates to a new social media account that had no mention of me having transitioned. I was just another fashion influencer pumping out content for their brand. I posted video and images of myself in the new styles as they arrived. My assistant had years of fashion experience and was gifted at visual marketing. I had grasped the numbers and was confident in knowing what it would take to make them move. We were a great team and got off to a great start.

Turnover is a given at all levels of the fashion industry. I was about to experience a worst-case scenario. My assistant was offered her own store with a brand where the visual layout and presentation of the trending styles was a priority. This was the right opportunity for her to take at the time. I was very pleased for her. She left quickly.

I barely had time to adjust when another one of my managers received the news of her mother's death. She would leave immediately to be a caregiver to her father. Another manager left the business shortly thereafter due to high fuel prices and a long commute that combined to crush her finances.

I had retired to have fun and learn the fashion industry, and now I received my first test of what the retail industry deals with daily. It was anything but fun. I hired the staff I needed to maintain the pace and get us through the summer and into the fall. But it about killed me to do it. We used the same customer-focused selling model as every other boutique within the brand. Brand leadership at the corporate level wanted that model utilized routinely; we just implemented it better than most. I loved it from the moment I agreed to join the team. It was simply focused on the customer experience. I wanted it done better than anyone else, and my team delivered. We met the customer on arrival, got the "deeper why," and funneled them to me. We routinely gave the customers a fashion experience that they wouldn't forget. They responded. The sales volume reflected it.

I entered my first holiday season in retail leadership, another one of those experiences I would give myself. The previous year didn't count, with consumer traffic being down due to the pandemic; 2020 was a lost year at retail. We cruised through the holiday with continued success. Despite staff "sickness" and work ethic issues, we finished the sales year poised to begin the coming fiscal year with high hopes. I accepted the resignations of half the management team as the year closed out—gladly. I needed a team that prioritized, understood, and loved what it meant to service the customers. So, I hired my customers.

My first hire was a woman I had styled and taken care of one evening when she needed a new pair of jeans. She was a retired police detective and could understand people better than they understood themselves. She was fascinated by me, my story, and the success in our boutique. When I needed a new assistant manager, I called Laura, pulling her from another brand. We balanced each other's strengths and weaknesses, and she remains one of my best friends to this day. She brought a young protege, Sam, with her to round out the core of the management team.

I added another customer, Margaret, an attorney who had sold her practice and loved the brand. A month into her tenure, we were visiting about our time at University of Oklahoma together. As we reminisced about the Greek system, Margaret was puzzled and asked why I kept referring to my time as a houseboy at the Pi Beta Phi sorority at OU. "I was a Pi Phi at OU and I don't understand why you keep saying you were a houseboy."

I finally understood the confusion. I responded with a smile, "Because I used to be a guy."

She looked me up and down and said, "Well done!" She couldn't have responded with anything nicer. We had worked together for weeks. My physical transition had been a clear success.

This wouldn't be the last time I would surprise a coworker. Every time I was validated in my appearance by strong women always felt like the first time. Being seen as a guy dressed as a woman is a fear that remains buried most of the time. I was blessed and grateful that I hadn't had to deal with the experience very often.

Meanwhile, the sales success continued. We had hit on something by focusing on the experience of the customer. An inquiry came down the management channel. "They want to know what you're doing. Put it simply." I responded promptly, "I make it an experience to shop with me." That was it. It *was* simple.

A financial analyst who was familiar with my sales success and history in pharma messaged me one evening. He asked, "My partner wants to know how you are increasing sales so much?"

His question led me to be more direct in my answer. "I changed associate behavior to the standard set by the company." Meaning, we simply maintained Customer Centric values. "The tasking in the store that runs counter to servicing the customers has been minimized," I continued. "I held associates accountable to the tardiness and attendance policy, terminating the number one sales associate when she called my bluff and resigned. Everyone believed me afterwards that I would do what I said. I told them they would be part of something amazing. I made it fun for everyone, took joy in every success, and accommodated every request for time and availability changes. I worked like a dog. Nobody works harder than me and they know it. They see me love on every customer that comes through the door and can see the resulting joy. No one can miss the sales increases at every level of management and the team takes great pride in it. I took away the distraction of individual sales data (there was no incentive for it to matter) and prioritized the results of the store."

As we talked about the future of retail and my future association with it, he left me with, "At a minimum, Andrea, this ought to be very interesting." We would stay in touch.

I figured out later what the true key ingredient in the secret sauce was. It was me and my experience. I was a great stylist, no doubt. But in three years, I had journeyed from a Harley-riding, cattle-ranching man who didn't turn any heads to a beautiful woman. I was the embodiment of a frog becoming a princess. This was not an exaggeration. I was quite confident that not a soul knew better than me what it was like to suddenly feel pretty, sometimes for the first time. I knew what balancing her look was about, the colors she would wear, the styles to wear, and what not to wear. And I made damn sure she knew how to wear them. I made it my mission to make sure that any woman who entered my boutique and gave me an opportunity to make an impact would get far more than she would've ever imagined before walking through our doors. In my eyes, there was no change too big for someone to make. I had lived the ultimate change. It was and still is my mission for the client to see their own changes with their own eyes.

In being offered the leadership role in WHBM Oklahoma City, I was also asked to be the face of the brand. I let that request and my success in that role go straight to my blonde head.

My move to fashion was a massive change within our marriage, and that was saying something. But it was certainly manageable. Our marriage had survived twenty years of amazing experiences. It was my reaction to the success of the physical transition that could be the last straw. The move was successful physically, and my constant searching for the next box to check off had waned. COVID-19 lockdowns had ended long before and the public response to me was better than I could've ever imagined before saying "yes" to the transition. Yet Summer and I hadn't been laughing, maximizing our time together, or connecting at a personal level for months.

Sensing a shift in her demeanor, I broached an important topic as we headed to the bedroom for the evening. I was sitting on the bed as Summer moved through her bedtime routine. Feeling the tension between us, I asked her, "You still love me?"

"I still love you," she responded. She was cool, and her answer held no affectionate emotion behind it.

My stomach bottomed out. "Are you going to leave me?"

"I don't know."

ELVIS SAVED US

I could've vomited.

"You've developed this, this, Andrea persona," Summer continued. "You never turn it off! It's selfish, superficial, the acting never stops. Not even at home! It's like the camera is always on you."

It was true. I was drowning in my need for validation. My feedback from my social media told me Andrea was likable. My followers gave me "likes." I was enjoying the new me. I was the star in my own show. But I wasn't separating from the need to do video for my job. I had a taste of seeing myself on camera and became gluttonous for more. This had nothing to do with my success in fashion. It was barely related to my transition.

Summer went on, "The core of your being is gone. You are buried in your phone, taking selfies. The transition isn't the problem. You're beautiful, but for me, this is just like middle school all over again. I've told you that the girls, the blonde-haired, blue-eyed girls treated me as if I were nothing!

"You get dressed in your chic fashion, then ask me to take photos of you to post! I'm struggling with this, doing my best, and having my face rubbed in it at every turn." Usually tears would be flowing in the outpouring of our pent-up emotions when either of us finally chose to open up. This time, she was past being sad.

I had not considered how my successful transition into the embodiment of her nightmares would affect her. We knew it would be hard. But it was past hard. And not for the reasons we had considered beforehand. I had promised to take care of her and I wasn't anywhere close to giving her what she needed as my wife. When I transitioned, I knew she wouldn't leave me. I had left *her*, with no recognition of the impact of my behavior on her struggle and self-image. I had given no thought to how she felt having lost her masculine husband to a blonde, wannabe supermodel. I was having fun with no thought of the impact of my behavior on her. This is humbling to write, and I'm ashamed. We went off to bed with our marriage at a low point.

My life had become like a movie where the plot has the average guy becoming the girl he writes up for himself. Summer had almost made the decision that when the school year was over, her part in the movie would end. It would take a scene from another movie to save our marriage.

We both loved Elvis Presley. I remembered watching his concert from Hawaii as a young boy. I would look at the vinyl record albums while my mother grocery shopped at the box store, and found myself staring at Elvis' *Greatest Hits* album. Mom eventually bought it for me, and I played it in her console repeatedly. Summer had received a CD set of his essential greatest hits for her thirteenth birthday. That gift deepened an affinity for him that had been fostered by her parents playing the album during her childhood. We would joke throughout our marriage about Elvis. She would say, "I love him more," and I would respond, "I've loved him longer."

Shortly after her revelation of the resentment she had for who I had become, she stated that she wanted to see the movie *Elvis* starring Austin Butler when it was released. "I want to see it, too. I'll go with you," I chimed in, not wanting to be left out. We made plans for the next week.

Another week in the fashion business, numerous photos and videos later, and I was completely blonde again. I was getting the next outfit together for a social media post, thinking about the camera equipment, lighting, and location of the shoot. I asked Summer, "Would you do a photoshoot for me tonight?"

With no reaction to me forgetting our date, she said, "Yep, but I have a deadline. I'm going to see Elvis."

I knew instantly what had just occurred. Everything she had told me came right back at me. It had gone in one ear and right out the other. The last three years condensed themselves into this two-sentence exchange. I immediately made myself ready for the movie, and we headed for the theatre.

The movie was great. The music wonderful. It was clear how fully enthralled Elvis was in his persona, his stardom, and his career. As the movie advanced to the scene at Graceland, Priscilla tells her husband she has given him everything. And he's not even a husband anymore. She has her bags. Crying, Elvis sits down on the stairs. Priscilla says she loves him, and leaves. He lets her.

I was sobbing. I was seeing myself, enthralled with my successful transition, following my wife out the door. Summer looked over at me during the scene and told me later, "I looked at you crying and I was sad for you, I felt bad for you, and I was still mad at you."

I had seen myself clearly on those stairs and I wasn't going to sit down. I would be better than Elvis. We knew the significance of the scene and my reaction to it. That night, Elvis saved us.

We came home, took joy in listening to his greatest hits, and I planned a trip for the two of us to visit Graceland. Over the next couple of months and after a few tough talks, we knew that the core of who I was had returned. The treasure found in the mirror and my transition wasn't the problem. I had failed to become a better version of myself. The girl staring back from the mirror—I had left her buried after taking the treasure. I had to experience being buried in myself to understand that while I was now outwardly reflecting an alignment with the new me, I had fallen short in my effort to be the person I aspired to be in my transition. I found that version in more listening, giving, gratitude, and understanding of those around me.

***

Summer rescued me. Her self-awareness, her acknowledgment of the pain she had endured, not once but twice, grounded me with the realization that the meaning and purpose of life is found in the experiencing of it. In all of our experiences over twenty years, we have found those things. In my transition, I had taken the opportunity to start a new life. There is still more meaning and purpose to be found in our life together.

Today, each of us tells those around us, "No one loves me like she does."

AFTERWORD

With my new team of previous customers at the boutique, tremendous success followed, and we delivered amazing experiences to women shopping for chic fashion in Oklahoma City. I was asked to lead a repeat performance in the Dallas–Fort Worth metroplex. I said "yes!"

I was met in Texas by a team with very little experience in fashion, but they could check every box in the demographic section of a job application. The laughter on that team saved my sanity. We became cohesive, efficient, and within six months, we were topping the previous year's results. Again, by delivering an experience to the women of Southlake, Texas.

During my time in fashion, I began saying "yes" to more experiences that would impact those who are lost in a world of social media. People are scrolling through on-screen lives that appear exciting, but while they inherently know there is more, they're not sure where to begin. One just has to say yes to maximize the potential of having a meaningful and exciting life.

Summer and I spoke for hours every day and maintained an apartment in Texas while I worked at WHBM Southlake. I returned home weekly to her, where our independence as individuals made us stronger when together. At home, I am whatever I am in the moment. I still do all the same things that I did before Andrea, just dressed differently and a little nicer. I'm quite sure I am the only woman mowing her own lawn in our upscale neighborhood. Summer ensured there would be no confusion on that point, or any other questions, by forbidding me to mow the lawn in a bandana instead of my hair. I did that only once. As our life continues to move forward, in reference to each other, we have wives. But with established friendships, we are "Andrea and Summer."

Damn, we love each other. The greatest gift that we give to each other regularly is the gift that allows the other to pursue what calls to the soul. We are secure in our love from one to another. It is extremely powerful. And, we talk about it.

Through the whole journey, I always have desired to maintain an intellectual honesty about my situation. I'm a woman who used to be a guy. Biologically born a male, with all the lab work indicating female. With men, I am completely comfortable, maybe more now, interestingly enough. But I'm not one of them anymore. I love connecting on the "masculine-weighted" subjects of sports, the military, and a wide variety of interests that we may share due to my diverse background. For those interactions, I am grateful. Remember, I wasn't unhappy before my transition.

With women, the response has been highly accepting and I live in tremendous gratitude. My personal connections are wonderfully natural, and I'm confident that the feeling is mutual. I know and understand that there are simply experiences that I cannot share with my female friends. That's perfectly fine. I don't feel as if I am missing or needing anything to have a wonderful life as a woman.

In public, there's little confusion with the "pretty tattoo lady," a label I've grown very comfortable with. For the outside observer, it appears much simpler than to me, the one living the experience. It's not an either/or, black or white. It's not simple. That's okay, too. I simply don't expect others to understand. It's not normal. Remember strength, toughness, sturdiness, assertiveness, and boldness? I live into those qualities daily.

My story is fascinating to read. It has been amazing to live. I'm so grateful for the journey. I left boutique management and moved back home to be with Summer. I was invited and joined LeadHERship Global and the C-Suite Network, executive leadership groups that impact lives on a global scale at the individual and organizational levels.

As a speaker, author, and coach, I find myself continually finding more meaning and purpose in life by simply living it, and encouraging others to join me by saying "yes" to new experiences. I speak to different groups about beliefs, expectations, and the divisions we create between and within ourselves that limit our ability to be the best versions of ourselves. I walk alongside individuals on their journeys to become complete, whole, and healthy by helping them to reintegrate and accept themselves.

It took twenty-five years, but I finally replaced the Corvette. And again, let it go. "Experiences, not stuff."

My transition was a sacrifice and a blessing. A sacrifice of the person my wife, family, and friends envisioned themselves with in their futures. A blessing to my wife, family, and new friends in ways of connecting with more love, patience, appreciation, and gratitude as time has moved forward.

I have been blessed with so many connections that want to be part of my journey and allow me to be part of theirs. The amount of gratitude I have for them is endless. The response and acceptance for me and my story humbles me. Team Andrea grows bigger every day. The journey has barely begun.

From Harley-riding, cattle-ranching husband, son, and father to rockstar female fashionista, I can testify that the most important things in life—like love, family, and football—can remain unchanged if we choose to move forward in acceptance of our differences.

REMNANTS OF A BOY

by Julane Borth

My first words when I looked at our baby boy
were *Isn't he the cutest baby you've ever seen*
I'm not just saying that because I'm his mother

he was perfect he grew to be the sweetest child
he was kind to his playmates he loved

GI Joe
Army toys
Hot Wheels
WWII books
Football players
Basketball games
Ronald Reagan
Moses
Jesus

that was a half century ago now she's happy
with mascara lipstick tattoos dresses
and high heels she looks like a model
in an office still decorated with footballs
war books remnants of a boy

I see her spirit her courage her heart
being perfectly herself

though transitions aren't always easy
often they're just right

ACKNOWLEDGMENTS

To my beautiful Summer, thank you for reliving these scenes over and over again, even when it hurt. Our belief in each other and the knowledge we share that no one else loves us like we love each other fills my heart.

To my mother, thank you for teaching me about the shadow, the masculine and feminine, and the process of individuation.

My editor, Alexandra O'Connell, you are blessing. Thank you for walking me through the process gently. You allowed me to stay in my zone of genius. Until next time.

Tremendous gratitude goes to my sister-in-law, Thumper Cooper, for being a listening ear to her sister and helping her maintain perspective. You reminded her that "boobs were included, and everybody loves boobs."

Thank you to my sister, Erin, for forgetting that I wasn't always a girl. Your acceptance was expected. You're amazing.

To Mason and Montana, thank you for the experiences.

Myron, thank you for keeping the hotline open. It's more important than you possibly know.

Linda Fisk, your ability to go straight to the core and believe in me instantly means everything. Thank you.

Tia Dawn Photography, you captured my alignment with a perfection I didn't know was possible.

To my colleagues, thank you for responding with acceptance, and you didn't even have to take sensitivity training.

To Tonya and my White House Black Market teams, thank you for understanding that it was always about the experience.

Melanie Carr, your dedication and desire to see Andrea Leigh make an impact is deeply appreciated.

Sara Miller, thank you for the joy you bring in service to Team Andrea.

Dr. Courtney Caplin, thank you. For everything. Dr. Erik Nuveen, thank you for your persistence, because you know what they say about boobs.

And to Dean McGee Eye Institute, thank you for the gift of sight.

Steph Brandl—two years of being inked in your chair, wow. Those sessions were transformative. Thank you for being a part of this journey.

To my sixth grade grammar instructor Mr. Morrow, who said I would thank him for the rigorous diagramming on the board and lessons on sentence structure, it gives me great joy to write that you were correct. Thank you!

ABOUT THE AUTHOR

Andrea Leigh is an award-winning speaker, transformational coach, and author. After more than three decades in the pharmaceutical industry, she followed her dream of working in fashion, becoming a thought leader in customer experience. Andrea now continues her work with clients, exploring personal transformation and reintegration through the individuation process, helping them become complete and whole individuals.

In this memoir, Andrea shares her journey, from long-distance triathlete, to embracing the challenge of managing her own homestead and grazing cattle, and ultimately the realignment of her identity—from Harley-riding professional guy to rock-star female fashionista.

The reader will see how Andrea's journey of self-discovery gave her the courage to say yes to new experiences, embrace disruption, and continue discovering the meaning of life through fully experiencing it.

Andrea and her wife, Summer, live in Oklahoma City, where they share in their passion for helping clients achieve wellness, healing, and self-actualization through their holistic approaches. To inquire about speaking opportunities for your university, corporation, or event, and to learn more about Andrea's work, visit AndreaLeigh.com